THE PAIN THAT HEALS
The Place of Suffering in the Growth of the Person
by
Martin Israel, M.B.

MOWBRAY
LONDON & OXFORD

Copyright © 1981 by Martin Israel

First published 1981 by Hodder & Stoughton Limited. This edition published
1983 by A.R. Mowbray & Co. Ltd, Saint Thomas House, Becket Street,
Oxford, OX1 1SJ

Israel, Martin
  The Pain That Heals.
  1. Suffering
  I. Title
  231'.8   BV4909

ISBN 0 264 66982 7

Printed in Great Britain by
Biddles Ltd, Guildford

See now that I, I am He, and there is
no God beside me: I put to death and
I keep alive, I wound and I heal;
there is no rescue from my grasp
                    (Deuteronomy 32:39)

For I reckon that the sufferings we
now endure bear no comparison with
the splendour, as yet unrevealed,
which is in store for us
                    (Romans 8:18)

My thanks are due to Denis Duncan for his help and guidance, to Tony Collins for many useful suggestions and to Sue Ryder for permission to publish the prayer found at Ravensbruck Concentration Camp.

The scripture quotations in this book are from the New English Bible.

Contents

Foreword

This book is a personal response to the amount of suffering that I have witnessed among the many to whom I have ministered and, even more starkly, in my own life. It has become obvious that the problem of evil in the face of a loving God is not to be solved at a purely intellectual level. The human mind, in grappling with this enigma, brings God down to its own level, thereby degrading Him and obscuring its own sight. On the contrary, it is by traversing the valley where death casts its long shadow that the sufferer learns basic truths about his condition. If he has the courage and the faith to proceed along the perilous path of self-discovery, he will come to the other side of life a changed person who knows God rather than merely believes in Him. For, as Pascal learned in his momentous illumination, the God of Abraham, Isaac and Jacob is of a different order from the God known to the philosophers.

In this strange life we grow through adversity rather than through success. The greatest lessons we have to learn are those concerned with loss, not gain. Although worldly wisdom emphasises the importance of winning the race to success and affluence, the spiritual path teaches us how to become good and gracious losers. The man who seeks his life will lose it when he dies, but the man who is prepared to lose everything he possesses for the sake of righteousness, enters a new field of experience that is completely at variance with anything he had previously glimpsed.

That these considerations are not entirely the fruits of individualistic piety is attested to by the situation of our world at the present time. Twenty years ago we were all living on the crest of a wave of idealistic as well as materialistic splendour.

The sky alone appeared to be the limit to our endeavours, and those who penetrated into the future saw marvellous technical advances in store for the human race. Today those who are attuned to the spiritual situation see disaster ahead as the world's resources crumble away and man's innate cruelty asserts itself once more in political and religious excesses in many countries. If we are to be saved from the power which God has given us, we will need to undergo that change in consciousness which is the precious gift of those who have learned the lesson of renunciation. As St Paul writes in II Corinthians 6:10: "In our sorrows we have always cause for joy; poor ourselves, we bring wealth to many; penniless we own the world."

This book asserts the creative potentiality of suffering and looks for a wider ministry of healing than that designed merely to smooth out life's difficulties. Its message will give cold comfort to those who want instant relief, but to those who are prepared to proceed with their difficulties with courage, it will show the way of advance that has been tried and proven by at least one traveller on the way.

1
The Many Faces of Pain

Misfortune strikes unexpectedly. When it does it draws us up with a start. The customary blind and heedless way of the barely conscious person is summarily interrupted, and a new focus of awareness is thrust, brutally and unceremoniously, before him. At one moment life appears to be agreeably limited to the pleasantries of surface concerns, while at the next a battle for survival has to be faced. The enemy may present itself as an illness, disappointment in relation to long cherished hopes, agonising news, or the maniacal fury of an assailant. If life's pain serves no better purpose, it at least makes us realise how little control we have over our own destiny and how greatly we are at the mercy of vast, untamed external forces — to say nothing of our own divided consciousness.

The human condition is not so much one of self-absorption as one of habitual preoccupation with a purposeless façade of ill-formed thoughts, charged with a variable emotional content, coursing ceaselessly through the mind. Most people would identify themselves simply with the individual whose life history they can record on an application form for new employment or for a passport. Many people's self-knowledge is limited to their physical body, which is their focus of identity. Their centre of consciousness fluctuates moment by moment, depending on the satisfaction of their bodies. This in turn depends on outer circumstances and the mood the person finds himself in at a particular moment.

The spiritual teachers of the world's great religious traditions frequently describe natural man as being in a state of "sleep". This is closely related to the concept of ignorance that is especially emphasised in the Hindu-Buddhist way. The

human being often functions simply as an intelligent animal —
sometimes not even a very intelligent one — until an unpleasant event disturbs the shallow equilibrium of his waking
consciousness. It is one of the fundamental contributions of
pain to make people wake up to a deeper quality of existence
and to seek evidence for meaning in their lives beyond the
immediate sensations that arrest their attention. But pain is
not only a great awakener. It is also a leveller of human beings
by its effect in dispelling the childish illusions to which we cling
in order to confirm our own importance.

The pain of the world has, however, deeper implications for
us about the nature of reality. We cannot escape the duality of
good and evil in the face of suffering. In the creation myth
described in the third chapter of the Book of Genesis, the
fruits of human disobedience to the laws of life are suffering
and death. These follow inevitably when man assumes a god-
like role as supreme arbiter of the knowledge of good and evil
although he lacks the transcendent omniscience of the One
who alone is truly real. To the woman Eve God said: "I will
increase your labour and your groaning, and in labour you
shall bear children." To the man Adam He said: "Accursed
be the ground on your account. With labour you shall win
food from it all the days of your life. It will grow thorns and
thistles for you, none but wild plants for you to eat. You shall
gain your bread by the sweat of your brow until you return to
the ground, for from it you were taken. Dust you are, to dust
you shall return."

This is an accurate account of natural man's life story. He
traverses a mosaic pavement of light and darkness, of joy and
woe as Blake puts it, but his end is predictable and irrevocable
and his passage is, as Psalm 103 reminds us, as transient and
inconsequential as that of the grass or the flowers of the field.
We plan and wait; we strive and build; we collect possessions
and seek to dominate our invironment, only to perish into
oblivion. Those who follow us care little even for our memory,
and it is in the nature of life that fools tend to succeed wise

men so that the noble edifices of the past are brought low. All is consumed in futility. And this, let it be noted, is the typical history of a person whose life has not been especially tragic. It follows then, as the Book of Ecclesiastes shows so clearly, that the natural human condition is "vanity". Human life, though it may have periods of surface glitter, is essentially dark. Until human consciousness has penetrated the veil of sensual satisfaction, which is the peak of materialistic aspiration, life itself is suffering to the one who sees clearly. Perhaps the Buddha has stated this fact most starkly, but it is not foreign to many of the world's spiritual teachers. This fact alone emphasises the necessity, indeed the inevitability, of the spiritual quest for people aspiring to an understanding of the meaning of life. Yet the spiritual quest intensifies our response to suffering until we are racked with the pain of all creation that was summed up in the life of the One who was crucified on the cross of universal ignorance and pain. Terrifying as this may appear, it nevertheless illuminates the human path with nobility of purpose and clear vision. It gives us the promise of a light that lies beyond the gathering darkness.

Physical Pain

The first experience of suffering that most of us have to endure is the pain that racks the body. None can escape its advent, for even the most insensitive person cannot ignore the calls and demands of the body. It is commonly said that physical pain is beneficial to us in that it serves to draw our attention to the source of disease within us. The message that something is amiss in a part of the body is transmitted to the brain which interprets the information in the form of pain, breathlessness, nausea, cough or some other unpleasant sensation. If this were the whole truth about pain, we would be justified in regarding it as essentially an ally with which we should learn to live quietly. However, the facts of disease are less simple than this. It is, for instance, the less serious complaints that are often particularly painful — a good example is the excruciating pain produced by a decaying tooth that has become inflamed and developed an abscess. Removing the tooth at once relieves the pain and cures the condition, which is, in any case, a testimony to the person's neglect of his dental hygiene. The condition would not have arisen had he paid more attention to the demands of his body. But the more serious diseases are usually painless until they are far advanced, at which time they may be beyond effective treatment. A particularly compelling example of this is cancer, which is notoriously silent during its formative period, but may cause severe unremitting pain later in its course when it has spread throughout the body. If only the early disease were equally painful when it was still localised, the attention of the patient would probably have prompted its investigation and treatment at a time when cure was feasible.

Furthermore, the pain of incurable disease may be so intense and unremitting as to deaden all normal human responses. Severe, continuous pain ceases to serve any useful function, since the disease is by this time so well established that no one can be oblivious of its existence. The patient becomes increasingly, necessarily dependent on pain-killing drugs which, except under the most expert use, tend to dull his sensitivity and awareness. This can be particularly unfortunate when death is approaching in that the patient is denied the important healing experience of the soul's transition into the life beyond death, its passage from the unreal to the real.

Severe pain of this type, if it is prolonged, is not to be commended as a way of spiritual growth. It cannot but concentrate the victim's full attention on his ailing body to the exclusion of all other considerations. This is indeed the immediate effect of any symptom of bodily disease, be it pain, breathlessness, or the disturbance of a function vital to full communication with the outside world, such as sight or hearing. Pain certainly enlightens the rather smug type of spiritual aspirant — whom we all contain within us — as to the superficiality of his dedication to God and his fellow men. As Satan said to God concerning Job, whom he was testing: "Skin for skin! There is nothing the man will grudge to save himself. But stretch out your hand and touch his bone and his flesh and see if he will not curse you to your face." While few of us would go to the lengths of actually cursing God, we would be sorely tempted to the corresponding negative action of turning our faces to the wall and dying without a struggle. Death is easier than life, and often more reassuring if you are one who rejects the possibility of survival of the personality after death, and believes in its total extinction when the brain perishes. In Sophocles' *Oedipus Rex*, the hero says: "Call no man fortunate who is not dead, for the dead alone are free from pain." To me even this statement shows a degree of unwarranted optimism, for I am persuaded that the dead can know the agony of total rejection that I find more terrible than anything we can envisage on this side of the grave. It is clear that we will never transcend the agony of pain until we have set out to learn its deeper lesson, the lesson of healing.

No matter how terrible the intensity of physical pain, it can at least be communicated to others. There are few who can stand idly by when an animal in pain whines and groans. The agony of the human counterpart pierces all those who have feelings of compassion. The Parable of the Good Samaritan is possibly the only teaching of Jesus that has been fully understood by His disciples, since its message is clear and the experiences described in it are of universal application. The heartlessness of the priest and Levite who passed by on the other side was, in all probability, a reflection not of malice but of unawareness. They were going about God's business, as they saw it, so officiously that they were blind to Him in the person of the victim of a brutal assault. They were asleep, as were also to be fair, Jesus' three closest disciples, at the hour of His most intense agony. But how many of us have the inner awareness to divine the agony that ravages the heart of someone whom we actually claim as our friend?

Mental Agony

Mental agony, with its appalling emotional overtones, is far more terrible than physical pain because it cannot be communicated to anyone — except the rare person who has himself traversed the darkness and emerged as a changed individual into the new light of understanding. Such a person is rare, because the worldly-wise avoid personal involvement with truth, preferring to listen to the smooth assurances of the spiritually blind leaders of society and the glib quoters of texts. These hide behind the barricades of their particular authority so as to be protected from a solitary encounter with the storms of life. Few people can bear more than a little reality — as T. S. Eliot remarks. But there is a time when we have to confront the full reality of our life, indeed of all life. This is when something we held dear is being removed from us. It may be a treasured possession, an ambition on which all our energies and hopes were centred, a deep personal relationship that is about to be severed by betrayal or death, or a metaphysical speculation that masqueraded as a living faith. Suddenly we realise that our lives have been devoted to an idol which we have mistaken for a reality. All that is left is an inner emptiness that seems destined to remain unfilled for ever. We are identified with the void within us. This is the moment of truth, the truth of our fundamental impotence. It can lead either to death or else to such a regeneration of the personality that a new life blossoms from the ashes of a past materialistic illusion on which we built the house that collapsed. But who can deliver us from the body doomed to death? St Paul sees that it is God alone, acting through Jesus Christ, who can do this. But how much do most of us know in our lives of God and Christ, even if we are sincere believers! Even our faith has to die every day if we are to tap its living springs, lest we confuse the faith with its source.

A particularly terrible part of mental pain is connected with its *moral* component. Perpetual awareness of guilt brings us to confront the judgement that is a vital part of the experiences of acceptance in a larger community. While some guilt is clearly morbid and due to manifestly psychological disturbances or baneful influences that derive from the person's childhood period, there is also a deeper stratum of guilt that is based on the overwhelming awareness of sin that is at the root of all separative existence. Sin reveals itself in the tendency of a person to fail to live up to the best he knows to be within himself, to fall continually short of the mark in personal relationships. It results from an ignorance about the truth of one's own being and of God, Who is the end of all our strivings. Jesus' commandment that we should be perfect in love and goodness as our heavenly Father's goodness is boundless, is an implicit indication that the knowledge of God is deeply placed in the *soul*, which can be defined in practical terms as the true self that shows itself especially during contemplation and at times when a moral decision has to be made. It is the inner organ of the soul, which is called the *spirit*, that has a knowledge of the divine; it informs us of our inadequacy and causes inner disquiet. Until we have acknowledged our failings, the worst wells up inside us in paroxysms of unbearable suffering that will continue until time, as we know it, ends. The greater the person's sensitivity, the more acute is his suffering. It is indeed a fearful thing to fall into the hands of the living God.

Another factor that leads to mental pain is unrelieved fear. Fear is a terrible cause of human suffering, especially the fear of rejection, for it provides a glimpse of the possible self-annihilation that all sensitive people must experience as part of life's test. I refer to the realisation of complete destruction that, at least rationally, may accompany death. The fear of rejection shows itself in earliest childhood in our response to punishment, especially that administered with apparently impersonal anger by an unloving figure in authority over us. It hovers over even the best of us in the ever-present fear of the loss of a loved one. Nor does life's race always go to the swift, nor the battle to the strong; "bread does not belong to the wise, nor wealth to the intelligent, nor success to the skilful. Time and chance govern all" (Ecclesiastes 9:11). Fear breeds jealousy when we compare our lot with that of those apparently more fortunate than we are. Jealousy is the cancer of the soul; it eats away all compassion and concern for things other than oneself, until it dominates the whole field of consciousness so that its victim is obsessed by one thought only. Indeed, the most destructive effect of pain lies in its tendency to evoke intense resentment towards other people, society at large, and especially God.

It should be said, however, that fear like physical pain, serves a beneficial function inasmuch as it promotes awareness and caution in the face of the bitter experience of past errors. The fear of God is indeed the beginning of wisdom; the love of God is the end of wisdom, and the whole purpose of life is to know that transformation of fear to love which is the gauge of the spiritually realised person. But the fear that saps the root of human consciousness is a dark negative force. It gnaws away at the joy of each present moment, sullying our personal relationships and destroying the fundamental unity that should be our experience in each instant of self-giving bliss when we stand outside the narrow confines of the person. It would seem that man's high calling to be a son of God brings him to an intimate knowledge of the realms of destruction and death, where he learns life's great truth in the depths of despair.

The human condition, seen in the light of reason, is a lonely one. Those to whom we attach ourselves emotionally soon pass from our sight as time and death fulfil their course, and our feeling of security proves to be an illusion swept away by the bitter events of life. As the Buddha saw so clearly, all that awaits us is ageing, disease and death. Suffering is the end of all life lived on a purely personal level, directed by the ego for its own satisfaction.

So long as man is limited to himself, he will be imprisoned in pain, the pain of the mounting loss of all that is dear to him which culminates in the agony of the awareness of imminent disintegration that prefigures annihilation.

Meditation

Give me the awareness, O Lord, to see beyond the surface of the people I meet in daily life and the compassion to share their deeper anxieties and frustrations.

2
Journey into Truth

When pain strikes, it overwhelms our placid assumptions about life and our place in it. It descends suddenly and occludes our accustomed vision. It drives us remorselessly into ourselves. We are imprisoned at once in our own mind and are forced to reflect on ourselves — the mechanism of our being, its origin and its destiny.

Suffering has an electrifying, concentrating effect on the mind. It becomes wholly occupied with one immediate concern, the self. Pain threatens our authority and our future independence. It forces us to guard our inner life against the inroads of destructive despair. Concentration on the self starts as an exclusive interest, and leads to selfishness at the cost of concern for others. The suffering person is occupied at first only with his own welfare, and looks for the support of all those around him. But even if this help is forthcoming, at least in the early stages of our suffering, the interest of others in our particular problem rapidly wanes. Most people soon recede from another's pain and suffering and prefer to occupy their attention with the surface things of life, as indeed did the sufferer before misfortune overtook him.

It is evident from this obvious account of normal human responses that suffering plays a vital role in our growth into deeper awareness. And the source of this awareness is to be found in the self. Many agencies that work to overcome the suffering of the world look to outer sources of relief, such as economic assistance or health projects. Necessary as these are, they merely scratch the surface of the problem. The cause lies deep in the soul of humanity; the outer discord is merely a symptom of a deep inner disease process, the failure to face reality and the tendency to worship idols.

Idolatry is denounced over and over again in the Old Testament. In those days, it seems, the ignorant heathen worshipped idols of wood and metal. Today we believe that, through the advent of enlightened scientific understanding and the spirituality of the world's higher religions, idolatry has been banished, at least from civilised societies. Unfortunately the facts are otherwise. Since the worship of natural objects has become unfashionable, man has instead bowed down to mental images, investing them with a god-like power. The form of this universal idol is the mind of man, which, it is believed, is capable of solving all difficulties through scientific research, economics, sociology, psychology, and the other branches of human endeavour. None of these disciplines is bad in itself; all are indeed gifts of the Holy Spirit who leads us progressively into greater truth about ourselves and the world we inhabit. It is when these disciplines assume autonomy, when they break free from their creative source, that they become demonic and start to dominate the world. Each in its own way, if dissociated from its eternal source, becomes a god, a power that dominates us. In this way suffering is seen in terms of its social, economic or psychological components instead of the groping of the soul of man from the illusion of material sufficiency to the goal of spiritual insight. Full spiritual insight is, of course, unattainable to mortal man, for when he reaches this he will be of god-like stature himself. What he needs is the wisdom that comes from increasing awareness, so that he can begin to direct his life properly and relate to his fellow beings as a person.

Suffering is to be seen as the result of a disharmony between the cosmic flow of life that is the gift of God's Holy Spirit and the will of God's rational creatures, by which is meant those endowed with a reasoning mind able to respond individually to that Spirit and co-operate with it. Those in our world are human beings, but it would be wrong to limit rational consciousness to the human mind; in the psychic realm there are also the souls of those who are progressing in a different medium of activity as well as the angelic powers. These aspects of reality become tangible to us only when we are capable of being released from the imprisonment of the ego by giving ourselves more fully to our fellow beings. In other words, love and service are the means whereby we come closer to the knowledge of God, who in turn, by the power of His Spirit, attunes us to other dimensions of communication. By an act of will, divorced from grace, it may be possible for a psychically sensitive person to effect temporary communication with this intermediate realm, but his contact with it is liable to be malevolent, since the spiritually uninstructed will attracts companions of its own moral stature. This is a universal spiritual law; suffering can be seen in this light as the way in which the will is chastened so that it may eventually be consecrated to the pursuit of that which is good. And we must remember in this context that Jesus Himself rejected the attribute of goodness, stating categorically that it was due to the Father alone (Mark 10:17–18).

It is fatuous to speak of the will and especially of the free will of natural man, for he is driven by powerful desires within himself and an overwhelming coercive force from without that derives from the world he inhabits and the society with which he has to come to terms. In this way what masquerades as a powerful will is, in reality, the enslaved psychic power of the personality which is harnessed to irrational inner urges and indifferent outer directives. To break this stranglehold on the personality so that it may become free and self-determining is one of the important goals in our life. But the end of this way is increasing loneliness (I John 2:15), for it demands a detachment from the assumptions of the worldly-wise and a strengthening of inner discrimination against the surface urges within the psyche that look for immediate sensual or emotional gratification.

Whenever a person consecrates himself to the spiritual path, which demands the subjection of the self to the full rigour of a religious discipline, he is evoking the will within himself — or perhaps it could more appropriately be said that the will is awakened and is consecrating itself to the pursuit of a new, higher way of life. It should be noted here that spiritual progress requires the discipline of a religious tradition. This alignment of the personality to a living faith anchors it to a body of aspiring believers and demands active participation in worship in a community whose concern is service for others besides themselves. By contrast, spiritual striving which is devoid of a living, communal faith usually ends up in idealistic fantasies devoid of practical fulfilment. There is consequently little growth of the personality into something of the stature of a living man seen fully in Christ.

The will is awakened and consecrated so that the person may become free to be himself. He ceases to be merely a faceless member of the mechanical society in which he lives, but starts to articulate his own identity. This does not mean that he excludes himself from the world so much as his little world no longer has a place for him in it. If one cannot conform to the demands of those around oneself, one becomes alienated from the society in which one lives and ultimately a positive threat to it, at least in its present form. The circumstance that usually precipitates this changed attitude of the individual is personal suffering. The man in pain is drawn up into himself and can no longer participate in the social dance. He is removed from the surface world and has to withdraw into his own being.

The theme of spiritual growth is one of withdrawal followed by return. But the person who returns after the harrowing withdrawal that follows great suffering is changed, and in turn brings that change to the world around him, so that it attains to a greater measure of reality. The experience of suffering effects the inner transformation that withdrawal demands. It is a withdrawal from everything that was held to be necessary for happiness, indeed for life itself. This includes material security, supporting relationships with other people, bodily health, and intellectual certainty. In any one instance some of these are likely to be threatened more than others, but each has to be challenged in a most radical fashion before it can be transfigured.

It is a basic spiritual insight that all we possess on a purely personal level has to be taken away from us before we can know that deeper inner authority that lives in a world beyond the changes of our mortal life. This is the first great lesson of pain. But this insight must be balanced by a positive acceptance of our possessions; they are not mere illusions but gifts that God has bestowed on us. Where we err is in clinging to them as a means of personal support and identification. Only when we have been obliged to part with them on this purely acquisitive basis can they in due course be returned to us, not as things to be grasped, but as treasures from God that are transformed by our love into objects of eternal beauty. As we change, so all that appertains to us changes also, and is brought back to God, transfigured and resurrected. Pain in its various forms is the great transfiguring power, but its severity is such that it shatters into fragments all who suffer except the chosen remnant that can stay its unnerving force with steadfast faith. This faith is a gift of the Holy Spirit, and its power is immeasurably augmented by the support of a loving community. At present, however, such a community is a distant vision rather than a practical reality, since, no matter how caring other people may be, they are weak in flesh and soon grow tired of supporting their fellows in pain. Only those who have passed through the valley of lonely suffering can be relied on to sustain their brothers in need. This is perhaps the greatest testimonial of a life well spent, that a person is capable of upholding the suffering world in the light of love. We must remember also that the one who can support even one sufferer is supporting the whole world. The work on the cross illustrates this eternally.

The question inevitably arises, and will recur as this account of suffering unfolds in the pages that follow, as to what part those who have not experienced any notable degree of inner pain can play in the life of the community. I would not like to make such people feel positively guilty because of the good fortune they have until now had the privilege of enjoying. I personally believe that we all have our quota of pain to endure; the heart knows its own bitterness (Proverbs 14:10), but it tends to keep this a secret until its outer façade is swept away by the inroads of misfortune. But while all goes well for us, let us give thanks to God in constant prayers of praise and gratitude, and be ever vigilant on behalf of those less fortunate than we are. The springs of enlightened social action depend on this awareness of God and of our fellow creatures. "Remember your Creator in the days of your youth, before the time of trouble comes and the years draw near when you will say, 'I see no purpose in them.' Remember Him before the sun and the light of day give place to darkness, before the moon and the stars grow dim, and the clouds return after the rain" (Ecclesiastes 12:1–2). If one remembers God with this intensity in all the circumstances of one's life, suffering will merge into happiness, and happiness be consummated in joy in that blessed state of equanimity which is the preserve of the world's saints.

Jesus tells his disciples: "If you dwell within the revelation I have brought, you will indeed be my disciples; you shall know the truth, and the truth shall set you free" (John 8:31–32). When the disciples claim hereditary freedom stemming from their ancestry with Abraham himself — that they have never been in slavery to any man — Jesus reminds them that true slavery is a state of subservience to the power of sin. Whenever we function at the superficial level of our personality, driven by the demands of the body and the ego power that directs it moment by moment, we are in danger of sin. While the body and the ego too are of divine origin, inasmuch as all things that are made come from the Father and the Word that issues eternally from Him, they can easily assume an independence of their own and be exalted to god-like eminence. They can dominate the person and eventually others also, soon assuming a demonic power. Sin is the result of separating oneself from the full flow of cosmic life, which one knows first of all in one's neighbour. The aim of the sinful life is to acquire things for oneself — sometimes also for one's predatory family — at the expense of the greater community. The end of the sinful life is isolation of the person from the flow of life. It follows that the Spirit of God, who is the lord and giver of life, is excluded from that person, who suffers a breakdown of health. No wonder the wages of sin are death (Romans 6:23). In this way, as Jesus teaches in the passage quoted above, the slave can have no permanent standing in the household.

The son, on the other hand, belongs to the household for ever. If the Son of God sets you free, you will indeed be free. This Son of God, seen historically in the form of Jesus, is also the eternal light of the soul, which is called the spirit of man. The light shines in the darkness of personal consciousness, but the darkness refuses its illumination because it prefers the surface glitter of illusion. But there comes a time in which this glitter, which is the vanity of life, is dulled, and the essential darkness of personal life is revealed. This is the moment of truth, when pain makes itself felt, and suffering is the one unassailable experience. Now at last the person is driven down into his own resources. All those advantages that derive from inheritance and experience fade into impotence, useful as they once were in the time of health and assurance. All that remains is the person himself. This consists not only of what was brought in from the time of conception but also what has been built through the experience of life's vicissitudes. And the power, or the cornerstone, from which, or on which, the personality has been fashioned, is the eternal spirit present in the apex of the soul of man.

Those who do not know this spirit are not only unaware of themselves as children of God, but are also unformed individuals. Their lives have lacked the warmth of full humanity, and the darkness of this extreme revelation is scarcely bearable. The pain that heralded this fearful glimpse of the destitute personality is also the only full awareness that is left to accompany the bereft person on his journey into hell. And it will be with him until he has allowed the Son full power in his life. Only then will he experience transformation, a return to life and full humanity. Pain is indeed the dark face of God, which has to be known no less than the brightness of God's love, in the full intensity of a personal relationship, before we can aspire to divine sonship.

When real tragedy enters the life of a previously unawakened person, there is at first a period of indignation and revolt, but with the unfolding of time he has to take stock of himself and face the new situation. There is darkness where once there was light, and the emotional darkness is destined never to leave the person's orbit until he himself is so changed as to be able to see the greater light through the darkness. In other words, the resolution of life's tragedy is not a blissful return to the *status quo*, to the old times of childish abandon and irresponsible indulgence. These are past recall. What lies ahead is solid labour in the darkness of cold reality, but the end in distant view is a transformed life. The greatest happiness that the human, in his natural state, can conceive, is a bliss of sensual comfort in which the ego, that point of immediate awareness which the person identifies with his true self, asserts its demands over the world, so that man himself is the measure of all things. This is an illusion that has to be dispelled before the eternal centre of truth in the personality can be revealed. When the person can function at this level of reality, he is free because he is no longer bound to any external source of support. He has attained a relationship with God, and comes to be increasingly full of the Holy Spirit as he confronts the mystery of God.

The cleft truth of the human situation therefore comprises both its divine origin and destiny and its terrible fall from divine knowledge in the course of incarnate life. This truth is in each of us. It is only when we acknowledge that there is something profoundly wrong with us in our present situation that we can start to move towards a total re-creation of our personality in the form of the divine nature that is deeply implanted within us. Pain in all its manifestations forces us to face this dark truth, that we are all become like a man who is unclean and all our righteous deeds are like a filthy rag (Isaiah 64:6).

Nor is our responsibility limited to the personal or even the human dimension. We, through our selfish way of life and abuse of the world's resources, have brought about a field of suffering that outdistances our conscious awareness of the damage we have done. I refer to the natural order of which we are essentially a part, though certainly the dominant member. We are in psychic communion with all life, and our own malalignment injures the relationship that prevails between all living beings. The tragedy of conflict in the natural order follows on man's conflict with God's creatures.

St Paul expands majestically on this theme in the eighth chapter of his Letter to the Romans (verses 18 to 22) in which he writes, "For I reckon that the sufferings we now endure bear no comparison with the splendour, as yet unrevealed, which is in store for us. For the created universe waits in eager expectation for God's sons to be revealed. It was made the victim of frustration, not by its own choice, but because of him who made it so; yet always there was hope, because the universe itself is to be freed from the shackles of mortality and enter upon the liberty and splendour of the children of God. Up to the present, we know, the whole created universe groans in all its parts as if in the pangs of childbirth."

Suffering is never entirely personal or isolated. In this thought we reach the intensity of the phenomenon and also glimpse its resolution.

Meditation
I thank you, O Lord, for the constant abrasiveness of life's encounters, which bring me closer to my true nature unadorned by fantasies and illusions.

3

The Dark Face of Reality

In analysing the deeper core of human nature it soon becomes apparent that, basically, there are two types of people: those who accept a spiritual world and those to whom anything appertaining to God is incomprehensible. The first group are not always better, finer or more admirable people than the second, but at least they can be assured of a starker, more authentic existence than is possible to those whose world is confined by the limits of the human mind. The rationalistic type of person lives in a closed universe in which nothing beyond the reach of the mind can be permitted to happen. The spiritually aware individual, on the other hand, inhabits an open world in which the apparently solid laws of physical science are being continually challenged and forced awry by external influences of a psychical and spiritual order. The rationally orientated person is scarcely alive to the challenge of reality: the spiritual person's life responds consciously to the universal law of the Spirit of God and is being led progressively into greater truth.

In this respect it is important to define the psychic and spiritual dimensions. The *psychic* includes all extrasensory communication between the mind, or psyche, of living forms, whether in our world or in the greater dimensions that lie beyond mortal understanding. In itself it is morally neutral, and is as likely to be mischievous as edifying. The *spiritual* appertains to the Deity, and is infused with the highest moral excellence, summarised by the supreme attribute of love. The spiritual mode is, nevertheless, transmitted psychically by the Holy Spirit to us human beings through the spirit to the soul, from which it is translated by intellectual precepts to the reasoning faculty and fed to the emotions.

It is, of course, possible for the spiritually blind to have the scales lifted from their eyes. Spiritual experience is needed for this to happen, and often this is precipitated by suffering. Even those who are aware of a spiritual world may have their sights limited to the domain of mere psychic illusion, which may provide a seductive means of escaping from the common duties of everyday life. They too have to deepen their understanding of reality by passing beyond the barrier of the ego to true self-awareness. This awareness is closely related to the darkness that complements the light of God. It is usually through the patient and courageous journey into darkness that God's light is revealed. But most of us would prefer to bask in the meretricious light of worldly comfort rather than move towards the source of all light, itself uncreated, that is of God.

This darkness is, in one respect, a cloud of unknowing which has to be entered into and penetrated in the faith of self-forgetfulness before reality can be touched. It requires an abandonment of all previously held opinions as well as the revision of worldly counsel. But it has a much more savage side also. It is a place of pain, of mutilation, which is not voluntarily entered into but into which one is forced by the trial of life itself. When one has put one's hand to the plough, as Jesus tells us, one must move forward. The one who keeps looking back is not fit for the kingdom of God (Luke 9:62). The movement forwards is, to be sure, one made voluntarily, by the full use of the freed will. And yet the path seems pre-ordained; it goes through a terrible wilderness.

When Jesus came of spiritual age, He submitted voluntarily to the baptism of John the Baptist. This was a baptism of repentance, of a change of heart. Jesus surely had no need of such a repentance. But in identifying Himself with His sinful compatriots, He affirmed His saving humanity authoritatively. Only then did the Holy Spirit descend fully on Him and the Father's approval was absolute. "Thou art my Son, my Beloved, on thee my favour rests" (Mark 1:11). After that the

Spirit sent Him away into the wilderness where He remained for forty days, tempted by Satan. The consecrated One has to come to terms with the darkness of life. The Spirit is His guide and friend, but also the one who leads Him into a deep relationship with the darkness of sin. This confrontation is primarily that of spiritual warfare, but the end is a tried, proved Jesus. Satan is also one of the heavenly court, as the Book of Job affirms; he too is created by God and is a child of God. Without the constant trial that comes from a living confrontation with evil, there can be no growth into the fullness of human life. There can, above all, be no living relationship with God.

In the creation story Adam and Eve live in a world of infantile perfection. They are one with life in all its forms and one also with God the Father. Yet they are unaware of the bliss that is theirs. They are living in the sleep of unawareness. It is only when they are touched by evil, symbolised by the serpent who too was made by God — though he is the craftiest of all God's wild creatures — that they know God fully as a being separate from themselves. This first authentic knowledge of God is both separative in content and dark in character. It is the wrath of God's law, now disregarded, that brings them into a fully creative relationship with God Himself. The way charted for them is bitter and savage, but it does affirm the authenticity and freedom of the human person, and promises, in the far distant future, redemption and restitution. Thus, paradoxically, the primeval sin of Adam and Eve, though it entails heartbreaking suffering, is to their ultimate advantage. The unfallen Adam cannot be credited with any sort of effective will, whereas after the fall the will is born, albeit tragically perverse.

"As in Adam all men die, so in Christ all will be brought to life" (I Corinthians 15:22). Indeed, the way of Adam's full recognition of himself as a human being with the perverse will that is a property of natural, unredeemed man is by disregarding God's command. This is the way of inevitable death for the person who functions, without regard for God's sovereignty, at the level of the ego. By this word ego, I am referring to a point of immediate awareness in the psyche that fluctuates minute by minute and is governed by the desire for immediate, continuous gratification. The unredeemed ego has to be slain before it can be resurrected as the servant of the true self, the soul that lies at the heart of the person. The ego is indeed the essential servant of the full person, but is demonic as a master.

Now Christ "did not come to be served but to serve", indeed "to give up His life as a ransom for many" (Mark 10:45). The ego whereby He shows Himself to the world in a continuous epiphany, or manifestation, until His death, is the servant of the divine nature within. And from outside it is the servant of mankind. The confrontation with the forces of darkness that commences after His baptism and reaches its fulfiment in the crucifixion, is the means whereby He shows his unitive knowledge of the Father, of an intensity far deeper than was His by right from the moment of His conception. Truly each man has to repeat the life of Christ before he can know God fully. In this respect the statement, "No man comes to the Father except by me" (John 14:6), otherwise so easily seen in exclusive terms, is manifestly true. Only by taking on the full burden of society's wickedness and the psychic darkness that rules the natural world can the aspirant come to a full realisation of that love which is the nature of God the Father and was demonstrated in the atonement wrought by Christ. In the paradox of unbearable suffering we come to the knowledge of God's love, for as we give love to the world, so we open ourselves fully to the source of all love, who is God. In so doing, we also affirm the divine nature in which we were originally formed and of which we begin to partake. In the life of any one of us this sequence of events is more likely merely to be started than completed, since our time here is but a moment in the vast expanse of the drama of creation. Nevertheless, life's essential task is always the same — establishing closer relationships with a widening circle of fellow creatures.

The darkness that surrounds God is the reverse side of His nature as light, for "God is light and in Him there is no darkness at all" (I John 1:5). But the world created by Him is separated from His essence by darkness of such intensity that only mystical prayer can penetrate it. Fortunately He is master of the darkness as well as the light of creation. "If I climb up to heaven, thou art there; if I make my bed in hell, again I find thee. If I take my flight to the frontiers of the morning or dwell at the limit of the western sea, even there thy hand will meet me and thy right hand will hold me fast. If I say, 'Surely darkness will steal over me, night will close round me', darkness is no darkness for thee, and night is luminous as day; to thee both dark and light are one" (Psalm 139: 8–12). The same thought appears in Isaiah 45: 6–7: "I am the Lord, there is no other; I make the light, I create darkness, author alike of prosperity and trouble. I, the Lord, do all these things." No doubt the darkness and trouble that harass us perpetually are brought about by secondary causes, but these too are in God's power. They will, like Satan, be our constant accuser in the heavenly court of justice until we have played our part in the transfiguration of the world, mediated primarily in the society in which we live. The very radiance of God's light blinds those who even glimpse it from afar in mystical illumination, until they have grown accustomed to it in a life given over to God's service.

Perhaps the most dramatic instance in Holy Scripture of the darkness and the light of God working in concert occurs in the story of Jacob's mysterious combat with the angel of the Lord in the depth of night. As will be recalled, Jacob's previous life was none too edifying. By artifice he had gained ascendancy over his brother Esau, and his dealings with his uncle Laban showed neither of them in a particularly good light. Admittedly Jacob was the less culpable of the two, but he had nevertheless left his uncle secretly, taking both his daughters and their children with him. Through divine intervention coming in the form of a dream, Laban is prevented from harming his nephew. However, Jacob has still to come to terms with his wronged brother Esau, now a powerful local chieftain. During the night Jacob sends his two wives, his eleven sons and his two slave girls across the gorge at the ford of Jabbok. Then he is left alone in the darkness. A man wrestles with him till daybreak. When the man sees that he cannot throw Jacob, he strikes him in the hollow of his thigh so that Jacob's thigh is dislocated while they wrestle. The man says: "Let me go, for day is breaking," but Jacob replies: "I will not let you go unless you bless me." He says to Jacob: "What is your name?" and he replies, "Jacob." The man says: "Your name shall no longer be Jacob, but Israel, because you strove with God and with men and prevailed." Jacob says: "Tell me, I pray you, your name." He replies: "Why do you ask my name?" but he gives him his blessing there. Jacob calls the place Peniel, "because," he says, "I have seen God face to face and my life is spared." The sun rose as Jacob passed through Penuel, limping because of his hip (Genesis 32:22–31).

To me this amazing incident speaks of Jacob having to confront the deepest recesses of his own inner nature, at once treacherous and courageous, timid and resourceful. Like Adam, but on a higher level of consciousness, he is asserting his identity as a person in making a positive response to the power of darkness which assails him and threatens his very life. All this occurs, significantly, when he is absolutely alone in the night. The accuser, who has a destructive quality, strikes when, in the dark hours, man's innate dread and awareness of his nothingness comes into terrifyingly clear focus. Jacob then has to face his inevitable destiny without the philosophical hope of immortality that comes to man with the dawning of day's light. But Jacob resisted the threat of the cataclysmic encounter, and would not yield. He maintained, indeed defended, not only his humanity but also his unique identity. The result of this supernatural encounter was reflected even on a bodily level by a hip put out of joint — a lasting testimony to the struggle. Something in him is irrevocably altered and he

bears its impress for the remainder of his life, in the same way
as the risen Christ bears the stigmata of His crucifixion even
when He appears to the disciples in His resurrection body.
What was a mark of extreme suffering now assumes the status
of a thing of glory.

In the story of Jacob's spiritual conflict with the dark and
the light of God's power, we see how his sins have become, as
Dame Julian of Norwich puts it, "No longer wounds but
worships". In so doing we likewise move beyond the consciousness of the superficial ego to the deeper self within, so
that an apparently new ego is born in us, one more closely
attuned to the spiritual self. No wonder, as Jesus tells
Nicodemus, a man has to be born over again before he can see
the kingdom of God (John 3:3). The baptism within always
embraces a sequence of inner death followed by a willed
resurrection, the will being directed to a nobler end outside
the person's own scheme of desires. "Put yourself at the
disposal of God, as dead men raised to life; yield your bodies
to Him as implements for doing right" (Romans 6:13).

The world of separation from God is the world of darkness.
It is a place of growth of the human soul into the knowledge of
truth, that man has to work out his own salvation in fear and
trembling, for it is God who works in us, inspiring both the
will and the deed for His own chosen purpose (Philippians
2:13). The divine source is never far from the one who travails
in spiritual darkness, because He is there within all of us in the
spirit that is the apex of the soul. But to most of us this
presence is more an act of religious faith than an intensity of
personal relationship. This is because the human mind is
incarcerated in a prison of self-centredness, and until it breaks
free from selfish limitations to a full participation in life, it
cannot know God in the intimacy that He brings. To know
God within needs an openness and willingness to give of
oneself freely and joyously to one's fellows. This is scarcely
conceivable until one has moved beyond the delusion of own-
ing any attribute with which one may have been endowed,

either by birth or by the world's acclaim. Only when we know that we are nothing and can rejoice in this knowledge can we give of ourselves without reserve to those around us. For in becoming nothing, one is close again to the Father like a little child, without personal power or guile, and one assumes something of divinity. In this state of grace we are at last open both to God and to the world, acting as a mediator between the two.

When tragedy strikes Job, despite his life of genuine charity and piety, he says: "Every terror that haunted me has caught up with me and all that I feared has come upon me" (Job 3:25). It often appears that our deepest fears have a strongly precognitive flavour — they seem to be inner warnings of a situation in store for us later on in our lives. But if we are strong in faith, we can call on a power beyond ourselves to sustain us as we approach this crisis period of our life. Jesus, in the Lord's Prayer, teaches us to ask God that we may not be brought to the test (Matthew 6:13). This is generally regarded as the most obscure part of the prayer. One possible meaning is that we should ask to be protected from the temptation of endangering our lives by precipitate and largely self-inflating actions aimed essentially at coveting a hero's death and martyrdom. In such a situation the unredeemed ego would be the master, glorifying itself in the fate it had itself fashioned.

In the real tests of life, over which we seldom have appreciable control, we grow into the knowledge of God in the dark obscurity of ignorance. He comes to us as an illumination that lights up every aspect of the personality, as He did Job's when rational argument was finally stilled in speculative futility. It is then, when all earthly hope is shattered, that the true salvation of inner healing is accomplished. In a very real way God has given man dominion over the earth, and men's darkness rules over living creatures, yet God does not interfere directly. His law will determine the fate of the world, whether it prevails or is destroyed. But until a living relationship is established between God and man, all human endeavours are consummated in destruction and chaos, the end being that primeval nothingness out of which creation was called forth. This living relationship between God and man is effected by prayer, which is the supreme human act.

The darkness that is the environment in which the sentient creature lives his life on earth (and presumably throughout the created universe) is to be seen, not so much as a part of the divine nature but as a property of the unhealed, untransformed world. The statement of St John already quoted that God is light, and in Him there is no darkness at all is true in terms of the nature of God, as many of the world's greatest mystics have attested. But in the world of separation, the world of growth in which we become perfect servants of God, the negative polarity of divine power, often called God's wrath, is essential for moving the creature on, lest he feels that he has arrived at a final state in which all problems are solved and in which perpetual rest can be enjoyed. Such a state would be a real hell, for there would be no knowledge of God as spirit and no growth of man into a spiritual being; in a way it would be even more terrible than the more conventional pictures of hell as a place of agony of frustration and self-accusation that are encountered in several of Christ's parables.

As the writer of the Letter to the Hebrews puts it: "All these persons died in faith. They were not yet in possession of the things promised, but they had seen them far ahead and hailed them, and confessed themselves no more than strangers or passing travellers on earth. Those who use such language show plainly that they are looking for a country of their own. If their hearts had been in the country they had left, they could have found opportunity to return. Instead, we find them longing for a better country — I mean, the heavenly one. That is why God is not ashamed to be called their God; for He has a city ready for them" (Hebrews 11:13–16). Admittedly this and subsequent passages refer to the prophets before Jesus, and we who come after have been acquainted with the supreme advent and the work of redemption He achieved by the power of love. But Jesus did not complete the healing work; indeed He is with us in travail until we, and also the whole created universe, partake fully of the divine nature in which we were created. This participation in divinity can never be applied from above; it has to be sought diligently from the heart of creation, whose spokesman in our world is the human conscience working in close communion with God. True love does not force itself on the beloved except by granting it complete freedom to be itself, and so have the right as well as the ability to make its own unimpeded choice. Dame Julian of Norwich speaks of the courtesy of our Lord. He respects the identity of each person with tender solicitude and leaves the decision to them. The way is open in Christ, who gives up His life as a ransom for many. But we have to follow the way, not shrinking from draining the cup that He once drained. But whereas He was alone in His agony, we are not abandoned since He is with us to the end of time. But it is only when the cup of darkness (which follows the Eucharistic cup of blessing) has been drained that we know Him more fully. In becoming nothing in the world's estimation, we become one with Him who was also discredited in the eyes of many, including those who were numbered among His disciples.

Needless to say this is not the path that natural man would traverse. He would prefer instant rest and comfort in an unfulfilled, indeed unformed, state. But the law of life is toil and travail. Until this burden has been borne with courage and faith, there can be no growth into the stature of full humanity, a humanity shown to us definitively in the person of Christ.

Meditation

Jesus said that while daylight lasts we must carry on the work of Him who sent Him; night comes when no one can work. While He is in the world He is the light of the world. But His presence is even more powerful when material light is dimmed.

4

A Devouring Fire

"For the Lord your God is a devouring fire" (Deuteronomy 4:24). Within this statement, repeated at the end of the twelfth chapter of the Letter to the Hebrews, there lies the heart of the destruction which renders growth possible. The fire of God, like earthly fire, both destroys and purifies. All that is ephemeral is consumed; all that is of permanent value is cleansed and refined so that it may be worthy of transmutation and resurrection. *I believe, finally, even what appears to be the ephemeral dross of much human aspiration is raised through apparent destruction to a realm of eternal value.*

False, or at least incomplete, identification is the fundamental error in human perception. When we are born, we are surrounded by an environment with which we identify ourselves quite naturally as soon as we are able to reflect as rational creatures. We have our parents, siblings and other relations, the home and its associations, and the social background into which we have been raised. As we become more aware of a point of inward identity — and this depends in no small measure on the way we have been accepted and loved during the formative years of our life — so we are able to separate or disengage ourselves from our environment, including our parents and close relatives, and start to establish that inner centre of reflection which is the soul or true self. This centre was in fact already present, in an embryonic form, from the time of our conception, but only as life is lived with full awareness can we articulate in total consciousness with the true self and work towards its greater development. On our success in attaining a complete relationship with the centre within, depends the authenticity of our life's witness, for it is the very basis of each individual's unique identity. And yet it is a paradox that the centre which we call "the soul" is also shared with our fellows to the extent that it is our means of communicating with other people and ultimately with the whole world. The soul substance of creation, eternally begotten of the Spirit of God, is universally distributed yet uniquely differentiated into those portions of consciousness that we call human beings — and doubtless other equally sentient beings elsewhere in the universe, including the indeterminate psychic realms.

Those who are to succeed in establishing their self-identity face much work. In fact their number is few, even among those living to an advanced age and dying at the close of a life of memorable outward achievement. This is because the things of this world tend to assume an autonomy in the lives of those who possess them; the power of domination inherent in worldly attributes overwhelms the possessor instead of their being used by him wisely and with detachment. In the end he is enslaved to the world and all it contains, so that, in his own eyes, his very existence is inconceivable without material support.

This situation is seen, in its most extreme degree, amongst those who live in affluent societies, for whom the acquisition of material possessions, once considered luxuries, is now an essential prerequisite for meaningful existence. According to the number of his possessions, so the unawakened person feels he belongs to the society in which he works. Where his treasure is, there will be his heart also (Matthew 6:20). If our identification is to be anchored to something that can withstand the pressures of daily life, a deeper core of identity has to be attained. The things of this world should not be disregarded, for they too are part of the divine creation, but they must be seen in their rightful place as something apart from us.

An even more powerful illusion in the quest for self-identification that dominates the lives of the unawakened is the sense of belonging that derives from personal relationships. The warm parental and sibling relationships of our early years are, if we are fortunate, succeeded by stable friendships with members of our peer group. This may finally flower in a marital relationship to be blessed with offspring that per- petuate one's name and provide comfort for one's old age. All this is, needless to say, acceptable in its own right, and yet the basis of much apparently ideal family life is purely selfish. To be sure, the personal ego appears to have dissipated itself in a web of loving relationships within the family, but this same family can easily become a predatory animal set on defending itself against the inroads of any stranger who might threaten its security, not only directly by competition, but also spiritu- ally by claiming its share of care and compassion. A time comes for all of us when the test of solitude has to be borne, as it did for Job when his fortune and family faded away and all that was left was ruin and disaster. Our lives all founder on the rocks of ruin no matter how noteworthy they may have been in terms of what the world calls success. That ruin encompasses three final facts of life: ageing, disease and death. Have we built an inner spiritual body around the eternal soul centre, or has our edifice been fashioned of worldly things that collapse at the full thrust of misfortune?

There are few people who are in such peace that they can dispense with the company of others around them. Few there are that can bear the silence of aloneness. From solitude they flinch in terror, and other people help to assuage their un- acknowledged emptiness with the froth of surface diversions. The centre of self-knowledge, the soul, is kept well-hidden in the meretricious light of worldly illusion. It is concealed by frivolity and entertainments which stimulate the emotions and confine our attention to the more acceptable realms of amusement and escape. To escape from a deeper relationship with the ground of one's being is the aim of all materialistic philosophies. The knowledge of this ground is painful and the progress to reality is precarious. The encounter with the deep centre within is painful because it is encompassed by a wound of extreme psychic sensitivity.

This wound, which is like a pre-ordained crack in the personality, is the inner manifestation of all our personal deficiencies, all the inadequacies that prevent us being full people. Furthermore, it is not merely of personal extent, for it involves all our fellows, all mankind, and indeed the whole created universe. In this wound of the soul, we know the inner Christ that is crucified for our own sins and the sins of the whole world. It tells us of the many times we, and all men, have fallen from the mark and preferred the lesser path of ego satisfaction to the greater way of personal wholeness in communion with all life. This inner wound that we all bear as a hereditary stigma is also a way to full self-knowledge and inner fulfilment. Its outer manifestation corresponds to what in depth psychology is called the "shadow", that aspect of inner negation which balances the outer image of well-being and success that we like to project on to the world. Indeed, the outer image of confidence is balanced by the inner reality of impotence that is hidden within the person who lacks self-knowledge. And it is this type of person who often rules the world, at least in his particular realm or discipline of training.

To know the true self, which alone is durable and partakes of eternal reality, requires a radical acceptance of ourselves as we really are, of the whole personality in fact. As the outer layers are recognised and put in their proper perspective, so the core, or centre, of the psyche is revealed. How radiant and warm is it, but how few of us know it! We are deterred from this knowledge by the surrounding layers of cold and darkness. Many people strive for this central place of warmth, of which they are intuitively aware and may even have touched momentarily in meditation or during some great aesthetic experience. But few will attain its full comfort until they have made the surrounding darkness their own possession also.

Speaking of meditation reminds us that are some techniques widely used at present, that aim at the achievement of a knowledge of the divine principle, the spirit, within the soul. Many such methods completely by-pass both the emotions and the reasoning faculty by the steady repetition of phrases or "mantras", and it is not unusual for the meditator to attain a state of inner calm and quiet. In this state the spirit may be encountered; this spirit of man, also called the spark or apex of the soul, is the domain within the total psyche where God is known, both immanent and transcendent. Unfortunately, this type of contact with the higher centre is only temporary; its transience is all too apparent, especially to those who know the meditator, for there is seldom a noticeable effect on his general level of spirituality. If anything, he becomes increasingly smug and self-contained as he progresses on his particular path, and seems to be less involved in bearing the tragedy of the world in his own life. Our inner feelings are often poor guides to our state of spiritual progress.

There are some mental techniques that act on the soul in much the same way as anaesthetic agents and pain-killing drugs act on the body. They may be invaluable during short periods of emergency, but they do not in any way get to the root of the problem or lead to the healing of the person. Often, on the contrary, the psyche will, in due course, hit back with all its emotional power that was previously suppressed and by-passed, and the effects on the person can be shatteringly intense.

It is the way of renunciation that leads us to the centre within, where God is known. The essence of renunciation is sacrifice, the voluntary giving up of something that is dear to us for a person or an ideal that is of even higher value. Jesus tells us that the gate that leads to life is small and the road narrow, and those who find it are few (Matthew 7:14). The narrowness of the path can accommodate the spirit only; our encumbrances have to be left behind. This is what renunciation means in practical living. The way to mastery of the self is through dedication to the highest we know. Unburdened by possessions, we are free agents and can traverse the dark terrain that surrounds the centre where God dwells within us. This is the form of meditation that brings us to God, not merely in an evanescent glimpse, but in full corporate unity, because the darkness is brought with us to the light within, and is transfigured by that light.

In the lives of most of us there is no burning desire to venture on this perilous journey, but a time comes when the soul can no longer be satisfied with surface comfort and is impelled by the spirit within to seek the heavenly kingdom. What appears to be a misfortune in the previously evenly-tempered life of a successful person is in all probability the thrust of the soul itself, bringing the person, despite himself, to a fuller realisation of God. In the famous words of St Augustine, "Thou has made us for Thyself, and our soul is restless till it rests in Thee," with which he opens his *Confessions*, there is acknowledged an impetus in the soul which will never allow it to rest in any country save that where God is known. This knowledge is one of unitive love that embraces all creation.

The thrusting activity of the soul is energised by the Holy Spirit, who works through the spirit of man to drive the whole person irresistibly forwards on the spiritual journey. In the Parable of the Prodigal Son, it was the spirit within him that bade the son leave the security of his patrimony and enter the wide, sinful world. When all the allurements of sensuality had been tasted and every possession stripped from him, only then could the young man experience the spirit in its divine authority. He came to himself and returned to his old home, but with a completely new outlook on reality and a changed attitude to life. Indeed, the relationship between the Spirit of God and the powers of evil is closer than our comfort would allow us to contemplate, but a time comes when even the most radical speculations have to be given expression, at least in our deepest imagination. The devouring fire of God, which divests us of all outer appurtenances, including those whom we believed were our friends, often shows itself in our lives more in the form of destructive evil than constructive good. He who can traverse the pit of darkness will emerge a stronger, more compassionate person. Nevertheless, even the one who appears to be over-whelmed in this life by the powers of darkness still has a place prepared for him in the life beyond death.

The journey to God is also the journey into hell. Before Jesus' resurrection, He descends into hell to redeem the souls of those whom the world has regarded as lost in damnation. I personally believe that this final descent was Jesus' great testing experience of love in the face of the intolerable dark-ness which He had tasted to the full on the psychic dimension during His agony in Gethsemane. Only when the entire underworld is illumined with the light of God can the Father be completely revealed; only by way of the Son can the Father be truly known. Our own descent into hell is a perilous, groping journey into the darkness of our own personality, which invests the spirit so closely that only the dedicated traveller through inner space can penetrate it. It is told in mythological terms, in Genesis 3, that when God drove Adam out of the Garden of Eden to till the ground from which he had been taken, He stationed cherubim and a whirling, flashing sword to the east of the garden to guard the way to the tree of life. There is indeed no easy way back to the knowledge of the centre where God dwells and where man was to know intimate union with Him. It is only through persistence and courage that the wrath of the guardian of the threshold of the heavenly garden can be assuaged, and man enter once more into his predestined home. There was indeed only One who could perform this enormous task, but through Him we too can venture into the dark wrath and begin to fulfil our destiny as sons of God.

When the darkness of the psyche is explored, an enormous power of evil is unleashed, and one has to come to terms with its high charge within oneself. Many sectarian religionists are obsessed by the great evil that dominates the world; this they conveniently project far from themselves on to other people of different religious views, or on to whole races or societies whom they suspect of destructive or degenerate tendencies.

The devil is to them a menacing external force who is to be combated ruthlessly until he is completely annihilated. "Awake! be on the alert! Your enemy the devil, like a roaring lion, prowls around looking for someone to devour. Stand up to him, firm in faith, and remember that your brother Christians are going through the same kinds of suffering while they are in the world" (i Peter 5:8–9). This admonition is apposite enough so long as we remember that the evil one is to be found first and foremost within ourselves. It is here that he has to be sought and confronted. Once we divest ourselves of him, at least in our rational consciousness (he can never be excluded from the unconscious depths of the psyche) and project him on to an external object of revulsion, he assumes demonic power and becomes an agent of terrible destruction. It is well attested in human history that more cruelty has been perpetrated in the name of religion than in any other sphere of human endeavour. When one includes such secular religions as fascism and communism in this saga of human bestiality, we can see how man reaches the depths of depravity when, paradoxically, he is seeking what he believes to be ultimate truth. The totalitarian type of personality, which dedicates itself absolutely to one particular path of human salvation, invariably becomes an agent of total destruction. The fanatical elements of the world's higher religions have around them the debris of human life, violated and destroyed, as a memorial to man's inability to attain divine knowledge until he has come to terms with the darkness inside his own psyche.

The fire of God brings us to the darkness within ourselves. It is an instrument of discrimination; it forces us to discern the hatred, the lust, the resentment, the jealousy, the unacknowledged selfishness within the deepest part of our own being. It leads us to see how every apparently noble endeavour or charitable concern with which we pride ourselves is tainted with unattractive elements of disdain and self-interest. It brings us to an awareness of the immense power of destruction that lies at the root of our personality. This is liable to be activated at any moment when our personal or communal security is threatened, but it is politely concealed under such convenient fictions as religion, patriotism, morality or public decency. There are few emotions more pleasurable than hating other people because we believe them to be a threat to public order. The demonic thrust of actions that tend to deny or thwart other people's enjoyment or way of self-expression is seen in the puritanism that raises its baneful head during the periods of extreme reaction that punctuate most types of religion.

Puritanism is, in essence, a way of avoiding the dangerous elements of life by occluding them from one's consciousness. The three ultimately threatening forces that are defined in religious thought are "the world, the flesh and the devil". Each of these is highly seductive, but none can in fact be avoided, because they are the very stuff of life. It seems strange to include the power of evil, which is personified as the devil, as part of life's substance, yet until its influence is accepted and worked through, constructively but unsentimentally, in one's own life, one will be deprived of immense psychic energy, and something both creative and dynamic will be excluded from one's personality. The shadow side of our personality is the receptacle of immense power, which, if used beneficially, could transform our lives and the world.

Furthermore, the Christian need not be afraid, for he affirms that his Lord has won the victory over sin. He should also, if he understands the theology of creation properly, know that God is master of all things, whatever moral quality His creatures have assigned to them. What God has created is good, very good indeed. Even the fall of man from intimate communion with his Father as a result of the perverse use of the will has not altered the fundamental goodness of creation or of the seed of God implanted in the soul of all men, no matter how corrupt and terrible their outer personalities may show themselves in the testing fire of mortal life. For there is a spark of the divine in all creatures, and until that spark is allowed to flame into a fire of purification and illumination, the dark side of the personality will prevail. "The light shines on in the dark, and the darkness has never mastered it" (John 1:5). That light is the eternal Word of God that lightens every man in the depth of his being, and came freely into the world in the incarnation of Christ (John 1:9). It devours all that is unclean, but even more significantly, it later returns all that it has taken up, renewed and beautified. What was unclean is now a source of radiance.

Meditation

Teach me, O Lord, to renounce myself daily in your service. Cleanse me of all unworthy desires except that of knowing you in the service of your son, Jesus Christ, even to the extent of entering the world's darkness and giving myself as a living sacrifice for the spread of your gospel of love.

5
The Hell Within

Hell has been conventionally portrayed as a place, a location, to which that part of the personality which survives death is consigned if the life led on earth was bad. It is presumably the mind-soul complex that would survive physical death, and since this has interwoven into it all our memories and emotional responses from earthly life, it would, logically, find itself in the psychic environment where it was most immediately at home. However, this view of the soul's departure is inadequate, and the picture of heaven and hell as places in the hereafter is far too simplistic. When Jakob Boehme was asked by a disciple where the soul went after death, he threw the question back by commenting: "It is not necessary for the soul to go any-where." Indeed, the soul is in eternal communion with God through the spirit within it, and, depending on how fully the spirit reveals itself in the life of a person, so his soul will know heaven and hell.

Hell then is a psychic atmosphere where the naked thrust of evil impinges itself on the bare soul, causing it intolerable pain that will persist until the person comes to himself and starts to repent. But what do we mean by evil?

As good a way as any of considering evil is to see it as the principle of negation, as that which denies the life-giving power of God and brings the creature back to the void of nothingness from which all creation was fashioned (Genesis 1:1–2). We do not need to go far to identify this nihilistic principle, because it is there in our own psyche. It shows itself as a forbidding, destructive power that casts its baneful shadow over all productive labour and creative relationships. It works towards the isolation of the personality, and its end is the disintegration and death of the person. And yet it is an integral part of life, for without its challenge and its perpetual witness to our inadequacy as people, there would be no growth of the person beyond static comfort to wider relationship with all living beings. In the world of form and multiplicity, good and evil work in intimate juxtaposition to stimulate movement and evolution of consciousness.

The Hindu trinity of divine essences, Brahma the creator, Vishnu the sustainer and Siva the destroyer, brings out this creative aspect of destruction very forcibly. Everything that is made has a finite existence in front of it; it has to pass away in order to give way to a new creation. But its passage is also illusory, for nothing that is created by God is obliterated. What passes on beyond our sight is transformed into something else, something that we will know when we too are changed. "The perishable must be clothed with immortality" (I Corinthians 15:52). We, alas, enclosed in mortal vision, can see destruction only in terms of loss, as that which has disappeared and can never be recalled except in memory. But if our lives were frozen into a finite mode, even one of the greatest happiness, they would soon become intolerable. Hell, in its ultimate manifestation, is an experience of complete insulation from all outer response, so that one lives a private life for ever with no other creature to care for one or even to be aware of one. No wonder the element of destruction is essential before a new birth can begin.

In Taoist philosophy, the creative essence of the Tao, the way of life, is portrayed as the eternal complementary action of the positive, directive principle of the Yang and the negative, receptive principle of the Yin. It is in the harmonious balance of opposite polarities that life's progress and creativity flourishes. Is this complementary action of the forces of creation and destruction destined to proceed eternally? The world of mulitiplicity — of growth, decay, death and rebirth — is one in which these two principles are perpetually interlocked. "The light shines on in the dark, and the darkness has never mastered it" (John 1:5). This is true enough, but the contrary proposition, that the light still has not mastered the world's darkness despite wonderful spiritual teachers and impressive higher religions, is equally undeniable. Indeed, these higher teachings, have, from time to time, been the source of such oppression in the hands of deranged followers that terrible darkness has accrued from the very religion that was founded to spread the light of God. It seems that the forces of light and darkness will be remorselessly in combat until the end of time.

On a purely philosophical level this solution may well be acceptable, if not inevitable, but all that is noble within the soul of man cries out against cruelty, hatred and injustice. It would seem that the world of separation, of multiplicity, of perpetual change, is not the final world. Beyond it, yet supporting it, is the realm of ultimate reality whose nature is divine, whose Name is unspoken but which is identified with the Godhead. Its experience is nirvanic; its end is the deification of all things, their assumption into God. But before this ultimate state can be grasped, there must be a full acknowledgement of the powers of negation. They must, paradoxically, not only be known for what they are, but they must also be given their credit, even their due of love. It is by the way of suffering that this terrain is entered upon and explored, because suffering soon tears off the mask of respectability that we show to the world and brings to the surface the inferno that rages within all of us.

When I speak of acknowledging, accepting, and finally loving even the powers of negation, the powers of evil, in our lives, I do not suggest that we can do this by a single-minded act of will. We love because God loved us first (I John 4:19), and only when we are infused with God's love can we flow out in love to all the powers of the universe. By that love alone can their final salvation come. Suffering is the means by which we are ultimately and fully open to God's love, though one must be realistic enough to see that only the few can respond in this positive way to the ego-shattering force of personal loss.

Suffering comprises two kinds of pain, the *outer* pain of loss and the *inner* pain of self-disclosure; it is this inner pain that follows the descent of the person into the inferno deep within himself. Indeed, it would be impossible to conceive any radical self-exploration that was not precipitated by suffering. That most searching of mind-exploring therapies, psychoanalysis, is seldom entered upon unless the life of the analysand has been so unsatisfactory that a complete re-appraisal of the psyche is accepted as a necessary part of its healing. The process of analysis has its terrible moments, but at least the support of the therapist is freely available. The autoanalysis wrought by intense suffering has to be borne, to a large extent, by the person himself, as Job discovered when he was confronted by the shallow sophistry of his three friends. Few outside the sufferer can begin to understand his dereliction, for the natural tendency is to flee away from any dark disclosure of the psyche. It is sad that even the trappings of religion and other allegedly spiritual agencies frequently are used to escape from the deep encounter with the self that is the essential prerequisite of the spiritual life. The first step in the authentically spiritual way is a journey into the wilderness whose lord is the devil, as the temptations of Jesus, immediately after His baptism and the descent on Him of the Holy Spirit, graphically attest. The spiritual baptism of lesser people is an experience of dereliction following some personal misfortune. In ourselves we experience the temptations that Jesus knew, and on our response depends our spiritual development.

The first interior revelation that suffering brings is to make us realise how lonely we are by nature. When all goes well with us we can admittedly lose ourselves in a heedless jumble of people whom we call our friends. But when we are suffering, these so-called friends disappear to leave us all alone. Thus after Jesus' betrayal into the hands of sinners, He was bereft of all His disciples who fled in horror and amazement. The man who was to be His successor as head of the community denied, on three successive occasions, ever having known Jesus. In this particular example of the unreliability of one's friends, fear of association with a dangerous and now apparently discredited public figure is the reason for their flight. In the more ordinary misfortunes that strike us, our acquaintances move away because they find any sort of trouble embarrassing in that it challenges both their own shaky equilibrium and the security on which it is based. Furthermore, the sufferer makes an implicit demand on other people's concern, and this is both time-consuming and threatening. We have, in fact, to come to terms with the truth that even when our efforts are flourishing, the human situation is one of loneliness, but good fortune can divert us from this understanding by filling our minds with surface attractions. When these are removed, we are forced to survey our natural condition with greater discernment.

It is possible to be isolated and alone even in the midst of a crowd of convivial acquaintances whose company one genuinely appreciates. It is a paradox of human relationships that we often use the companionship of other people to escape contact with the dark void that lies deep within us, and consequently to avoid any deep communication with them also. Conversation is often a deceptive way of escaping from a real communion with other people; a barrage of empty words can shield us from the inner scrutiny that truth demands. True communication consists in giving of oneself to another person in the deepest concern; this necessitates giving of one's full attention to that person from the depths of one's consciousness. Only when the inferno within oneself is known and mastered can one communicate from one's depths to another person. This inner hell is solitary in terms of human companionship, but it contains a milling throng of demons that inhabit the deepest recesses of the mind. Their master is the spirit of fear, around which they cluster "prowling around looking for someone to devour" in the words that have already been quoted from St Peter's first Letter. The ones particularly in danger of being devoured by the demons within are those of our associates whose lives appear to be successful and happy. The demons rejoice in the names of anger, hatred, jealousy and a deep desire for annihilation both of the self and the world.

It is terrifying to discover how superficially placed these destructive emotions are within the psyche. Whenever we are thwarted, they come to the surface to assert our own frustration. Furthermore, they have to be acknowledged; the psychological mechanism of repression simply confines them to the deeper part of the psyche where they can involve themselves in a much more dangerous subversion of the whole personality. The psychic energy they unleash will then be used against the body and produce diseases of psychosomatic origin. It may be necessary to suppress these emotions temporarily, but in due course they have to be faced and acknowledged. We soon realise that only a small part of the personality has really grown up into adulthood. We contain within us powerful forces that behave like the spoilt children we once were; they rage against the world if they are not immediately and completely satisfied.

Anger follows the frustration of our plans and ambitions. It is aligned to the concept of justice and is often called righteous indignation. When we are righteously indignant about an injustice wrought against ourselves — or more particularly against someone else about whom we are deeply concerned — by some external human agency, there is often a genuine desire for God's justice to be vindicated. But when the anger is over the frustration of our schemes by impersonal forces of misfortune, our fury is directed basically against life itself, or even more positively, against the author of life and justice, whom we call God. To be angry with God is not reprehensible. Neither Job nor the Psalmist restrains his anxiety over God's hiddenness in so much of the travail of human life, nor his anger over the apparent misfortunes that harry the way of the righteous man. In the confessions of Jeremiah that are scattered through the account of his prophetic ministry, he speaks in harsh, direct terms about God's intrusion into his private life.

"Alas, alas my mother, that you ever gave me birth! A man doomed to strife, with the whole world against me. I have borrowed from no one, I have lent to no one, yet all men abuse me . . . Why then is my pain unending, my wound desperate and incurable? Thou art to me like a brook that is not to be trusted, whose waters fail." To all this complaint in Jeremiah 15:10–18, God simply tells the prophet to stop grumbling and get on with his work. "If you will turn back to me, I will take you back and you shall stand before me. If you choose noble utterance and reject the base, you shall be my spokesman" (verse 19). Later on Jeremiah says of God: "O Lord, thou hast duped me, and I have been the dupe; thou hast outwitted me and hast prevailed" (Jeremiah 20:7). He curses the day he was born, as Job, probably constructed fictionally on the life of Jeremiah, also does at the beginning of his debate with his three friends. The life of Jeremiah is one long saga of suffering in order to bring the word of God to a heedless people whose doom appears to have been predestined — as may well be the case in our generation also.

Anger becomes demonic when it severs its connection with reason and becomes purely destructive. Then it enters the phase of black hatred against another person, or society, or life itself. It longs for destruction, and is the author of persecution and massacre. Much apparently praiseworthy criticism against the abuses of society is based more on hatred than on love. To project our own sense of grievance against some class of society whom we personally detest, because it possesses attributes that we lack, is particularly enjoyable if we can do this in the name of solidarity with the downtrodden and oppressed. Only the minority of social reformers are motivated primarily by the spirit of charity and compassion; the majority are impelled by a deep hatred of the prevailing establishment. It is no wonder that governments dedicated to social reform tend to become even more oppressive and tyrannical than those they so recently supplanted. Even permissiveness in sexual morality can be a protest at the restraints of past discipline rather than a genuine concern for those whose way of life is aberrant, and who need unreserved acceptance in love.

Suffering has the virtue of bringing us to face the demonic anger and hatred that energises so much of our psyche. At first these emotions run riot throughout the personality, but in due course they are brought under control because they are seen to be unavailing. A child's tantrums may be appeased by its parents' tender solicitude, but an adult's rage simply estranges his fellows and separates himself even more completely from God. Thus prolonged suffering brings us to the truth of our native condition, that of a selfish child parading itself in the body and concepts of an adult. It also shows us how much we resent the prosperity of other people when we ourselves are in distress. The core of jealousy within us is easily masked by pious attitudes when all is going well, but when our own security is threatened, we soon lash out at others.

A variant of anger is jealousy. It should be distinguished from envy, which though equally unacceptable, is not so destructive as jealousy. The envious person desires and inwardly covets those attributes of someone whom he considers more fortunate than himself. The first stage of envy is often one of admiration, which in itself is unexceptionable. But this is followed by the insidious tendency to compare oneself with the person who is the object of one's attraction, seeing oneself as inferior to him and resenting that inferiority. The next stage in this process of inner covetousness is that of dwelling upon and even assuming the attribute in one's own imagination. This causes great suffering because the fantasy cannot be realised in outer life. In due course, if the envy is not healed by a growing maturity of understanding as to the limited nature of all talents and abilities in the reality of life, there is a descent to jealousy. Here the covetousness of envy is allied to the destructiveness of hatred. There is a mounting desire to disparage the person who is envied, to show that he too has feet of clay. Aspersions are cast on his integrity and his private life, and he is subtly diminished. The unobtrusive evil of mischief-making works towards the total demolition of the one who is envied. There is no more terrible cancer of the soul than jealousy; it eats away all other concerns and interests until it dominates the full range of consciousness. It erodes relationships by destroying all that is noble and compassionate in the darkness of hatred and malice.

It is interesting how even the mechanism of envy is a perversion of a potentially beneficial attitude, that of the way of spiritual growth of a younger person who moulds his life upon that of a revered teacher. Both the envious person and the disciple of an esteemed master imbibe the desired qualities deeply in their own imagination. For instance, the imitation of the qualities of Jesus is a recognised way of progress in the Christian life. But whereas the disciple acts in humility, love and self-sacrifice to the higher ideal, the envious person appropriates the attributes in his imagination in order to boost his poor opinion of himself and inflate his weakly developed personality. He does not grow in spiritual proficiency, and remains obsessed by the great gulf that lies between the ideal vainly imagined and the reality that lies within himself. Since he cannot attain what he seeks, he becomes increasingly imprisoned in his own impotence, so that his thoughts are totally concentrated on his lack. It should be noted, in passing, that this is also a hazard in the development of those devotees who model their lives upon that of an idealised master of the spiritual way. Indeed, this approach to spirituality has only a limited value despite the stress laid upon it in a number of religious traditions. An experienced spiritual director will guide his pupil's devotion to God along the unique way of that disciple, while he keeps himself discreetly in the background.

The end of the hatred that blazes forth in anger and jealousy is a desire for annihilation of the world and of the person himself. When Job was tested to the point of losing his self-respect by developing a repulsive skin disease, his wife told him to curse God and die. Job admittedly chided her, reminding her that good and evil both come from God, and we are bound to accept both as part of our lives on earth. But then he, like Jeremiah, cursed the day of his birth and longed for death. As far as we know, the writer of the book of Job had no scheme of survival of death to anticipate other than an insubstantial wraith-like existence in Sheol. This would probably be a vain shadow life devoid of action, relationships and future hope.

Whenever a person behaves abominably to his fellows, we should spare him a prayer instead of merely judging him according to his actions. Those whose own lives are unhappy bring unhappiness upon others with whom they communicate whether in their home or at work. It is a way of relieving one's own suffering to visit at least some of it on to other people. Of course this is an entirely negative mechanism of unburdening oneself, and its logical conclusion is destruction of everything around one, including oneself. Race hatred, religious intolerance, and fear of strangers are all testimonials to the inner turmoil of those who profess these destructive social attitudes. They can, to some extent, be relieved by attending to the adverse social conditions that cause men to fight against their neighbours in the guise of self-preservation. But the root of this hatred that would destroy all others who pose a threat to our own flimsy existence, lies in ourselves. Until we as individuals have come to a solid core of inner reality which is the centre of the soul, we will always equate inner security with outer possessions, be they money, prosperity, social position, intellectual proficiency or even bodily health. While all of these are of the utmost importance in our lives, especially health of body and mind, none can be reckoned on indefinitely. Suffering may have to render us naked of every one of these appurtenances, including also our treasured relationships with other people, before we can attain a knowledge of the one thing needful for salvation, the word of God that is deeply implanted in the soul where the spirit joins us to Him eternally.

The complete process may be summarised thus. The natural life of a heedless man is one of unconscious selfishness. The life of suffering that, in due course, ensues is one of intensified, morbid selfishness, but the person is no longer heedless. The end of suffering is the total destruction of the selfish personal ego as the soul is broached and its spirit now informs the personality and controls the life of the person.

But it must be acknowledged that this third phase is seldom attained in this life on earth. At most it can be glimpsed as the way of progress in the life beyond death.

Meditation

Whenever I feel especially hostile to another person or revolted by an event in the world around me, may my gaze be directed inwards to see the flaw in my own personality and to offer it to God in prayer. Only then can I be worthy of offering myself as an agent of reconciliation and healing.

6

An Encounter with Fear

The demonic throng that inhabits the inner recesses of the mind is dominated by the spirit of fear. Fear is the inveterate enemy of progress in the lives of people. It immobilises us, allowing us neither to proceed upon our proper course, nor letting us investigate the world around us. It paralyses our endeavours and leads us to choose the *status quo*, the present situation, as the best for us, since it impresses upon us the conviction that any movement away from it is fraught with intolerable hazards.

Fear can be seen as the negative polarity of the virtues of prudence and providence. The prudent person looks before he takes a further step. He investigates the disadvantages of a course of action as well as its attractions. He waits for a propitious moment before venturing on a well-devised scheme of action. In the same spirit of responsibility, the provident person shows foresight in his expenditure of money and other resources. He knows the value of all created things and is a mirror in his own life of the divine providence of God. But neither prudence nor providence paralyses a person; they merely check impetuous attitudes that show themselves in the ill-considered actions and hasty words that we learn subsequently to regret. For once any thought or attitude escapes from the mind of the person who harbours it, it issues forth in deeds and words that can never be called back. Indeed, perverse thoughts themselves, if they are not contained in a morally orientated mind that is in prayerful communion with God, can affect the psychic atmosphere of the world, and lead to grave aberrations on the part of unduly sensitive, receptive people. It might be wondered how a mind in prayerful communion with God could harbour bad thoughts, but we have already seen how the darkness of the unconscious surrounds the light of the soul in which the spark of God burns eternally. The demons of the darkness issue forth as destructive thoughts with potent emotional charge, especially in times of severe suffering. Those who have the benefit of an active prayer life will not find themselves immune from the explosion of inner violence, but they are able to contain the charge by lifting it up to God. This is the way of transmutation that is a vitally important part of the ascent from darkness to light.

As I have already said, however, it is when perverse attitudes are actualised in deeds and words that their power assumes destructive proportions. They then can no longer be concealed within the psyche of the person but become elements of general psychic commerce. "Make no mistake about this: God is not to be fooled; a man reaps what he sows. If he sows seed in the field of his lower nature, he will reap from it a harvest of corruption, but if he sows in the field of the Spirit, the Spirit will bring a harvest of eternal life" (Galatians 6:7–8). The fruits of action, or karma in the Hindu-Buddhist tradition, are indeed irrevocable. They are the bricks and mortar of the edifice of suffering, and their transfiguration is the way of release from mortality to eternal life.

The virtues of prudence and providence cut down in this way the baneful karma, the fruit of ill-considered action, that selfish, unwise styles of living bring in their train. But when they reach an intensity such as to restrict the life of a person, so that he is prevented from going out into the world as an independent individual, they degenerate into fear. At this point there is no growth, and in any living system a failure to grow brings with it an ever-increasing tendency towards attrition and death. This is indeed the end of our physical bodies that have been fashioned with only a finite lifespan in view. But we have reason to believe that a deeper, more interiorly placed soul principle grows in experience even when the body disintegrates, and will indeed, "on the last day", see the resurrection of all physical matter into spiritual radiance.

Fear depletes the soul of its radiance, and leads the body to a premature withering through disuse.

Whereas the prudent, provident person is informed by a sense of purpose, so that he husbands his resources with care and skill for the day of enterprise in the future, the person racked with fear clings desperately to the little he has, seeing only diminution and destruction ahead of him. Even if his "little" is in fact a vast fortune by the world's standards, it is still a pitiful accumulation insofar as it is of help to him. It is no great paradox that some millionaires are amongst the least happy people we know, whereas a widow with her mite's subsistence-allowance may be a focus of blessing for all those around her. The millionaire's identity revolves around his wealth; the widow's identity radiates from her soul, which is immortal. "Though our outward humanity is in decay, yet day by day we are inwardly renewed" (II Corinthians 4:16). But this renewal depends on an awareness of God and our cease-less communion with Him in prayer. It is not to be seen as an automatic process any more than we can take our physical health for granted if we fail to obey the elementary laws of hygiene.

In the Parable of the Talents (Matthew 25:14–30), the kingdom of heaven is composed of those who use the gifts that God has given them. They reap their reward through their prudent and resourceful service. We all have to take risks, but if we use the inner gifts of discernment and intuition with which we have been endowed, we will come through the necessary perils of life in victory, and enter into our Master's delight. But the one who buries his talent in fear of its con-sequences is flung out into the darkness of hell. This terrible fate is to be seen not so much a punishment for an ill-used life as the inevitable result of living such a life. If we do not live our lives with purpose and courage, our personality does not grow. What does not grow declines and wastes away until all that remains is a dark, disintegrated chaos of conflicting attri-butes that were once the bricks and mortar of our personality.

In other words, the life we lead is our immediate judge, with God in Christ as our advocate and healer when we eventually come to ourselves and begin to live properly.

Yet no one can come to an authentic knowledge of love except through fear; the full providence of God is known only to the person who is so distracted with fear that he is forced to open himself to the undemanding love of God. While providence and prudence are worldly virtues that ensure a well-ordered, prosperous life during times of equity and peace, it is by way of the darkness of paralysing fear that we pass beyond the desire for success to a knowledge of God in failure, that God Who is perpetually crucified until all men are lifted up to Him. What then is this fear and how does it originate?

Fear is, in essence, the result of an encounter with the other side of being, that which is not oneself, which is vast, all-pervading, and annihilating in tendency. As soon as a baby is born, it cries. Its cry is of distress, even terror; it is not one of the joy inherent in being born into the world. The infant has left the safe, evenly-conditioned confines of its mother's womb for the cold, indifferent, outer world. But even more terrifying than this change in physical environment is the dark psychic atmosphere in which the little child is now immersed. At first it is protected against the full force of this destructive influence that pervades the world of thought and emotion by the solicitude and love of those caring for it — if indeed such care is available. But it soon learns that this love is not to be taken for granted; it is not unconditional but depends on its own attitude and behaviour, first to its parents and later on to its peers and teachers. Once it arouses their antagonism, it will soon become aware of the frightening negative emotions of irritation and aversion. The end-product of this active dislike is punishment. In this way the law of cause and effect is learnt at a tender age: a man reaps what he sows. Sometimes, however, the seeds of disobedience sown by a small child are out of all proportion to the harvest of brutality reaped, because there are some people who are unbalanced psychologically, if not permanently then at least periodically during phases of physical or mental suffering. The negative emotions emanating from unhappy people add to the boundless psychic darkness that envelops our fallen world, and a small child is much more vulnerable to the impact of this destructive emotional force than he would be in later life, when he would have had the time and opportunity to develop the rational side of his personality. The young, in common with animals and the primitive peoples of the world, are extremely receptive to psychic impulses since they have not yet developed a strong ego consciousness. The ego, though destructive as the master of the person, is an essential part of the personality. When used properly, it is the soul's servant, and it protects the person against the invasion of harmful psychic impulses arising from outside. Without its constant presence, the psyche is liable to be flooded by the fearsome emanations that derive from purely human sources as well as the deeper, vaster psychic world in which we live our interior experiences. The revulsion we experience quite spontaneously when in the company of an emotionally disordered person who emits venom at those around him, even if we ourselves are detached from him in relationship and have no connection with his hatred, is due to the force of psychic evil that is channelled through him, and is an aspect of the darkness that pervades the inner world of our lives.

Fortunately this is not the complete picture, otherwise the whole human race would be lost in the infernal darkness that surrounds and envelops it. The psychic realm also contains beneficent forces in the form of the angelic hierarchy and the communion of saints, those great souls, some of whom we may have known in the flesh as our friends, who are about God's business in lightening the darkness of the psychical world and bringing protection and love to us who are so often bewildered and distraught with suffering. In the words of the writer of the Letter to the Hebrews (12:22–24), "the fully committed stand before Mount Zion and the city of the living God, heavenly Jerusalem, before myriads of angels, the full concourse and assembly of the first-born citizens of heaven, and God the judge of all, and the spirits of good men made perfect, and Jesus the mediator of a new covenant." It is these who illuminate the darkness of hell until it attains the glorious consummation of all things in God, when all duality is taken up into the unity of the Godhead. Jesus too teaches us never to despise one of those little ones, for they have their guardian angels in heaven, who look continually on the face of our heavenly father (Matthew 18:10).

Indeed, the small child with his pure psychic sensitivity is closer both to the angels and the destructive demonic forces than are its older brethren. The greater the acceptance and love the child receives, the closer is it linked to the forces of light; the more it is ignored and rejected, the more tenuous is its awareness of God and the more deeply is it immersed in the darkness of negation. Whenever a cloud of anger passes over an adult's face, the small child absorbs the force of the emotion, and it experiences the fear of punishment and rejection. Inasmuch as this awareness of psychic darkness, which brings with it the negative emotional response of fear, teaches the child the basic code of acceptable social behaviour, it has its place in the maintenance of order and the concern for other people's feelings. The fear of the Lord is, as the sages of Israel repeated in the Old Testament books, the beginning of wisdom. If a person turns away from the morally acceptable path, he excludes himself increasingly from his fellows and ends up in such complete isolation that the darkness becomes unbearable. Then he may be available to conversion.

But there is a much more sinister fear that overwhelms the person to the point of annihilation. This follows cruel, unjust treatment by evil people on a faceless victim. The worst examples of this vicious evil in our own century have been seen in totalitarian prison camps, the purpose of which has been to reduce the identity of subject people relentlessly to total disintegration. This is indeed the final test that we all, in our own way and time, will have to endure before we are able to discover and affirm the one principle within ourselves that cannot be extinguished — the spirit of the soul. It comes about in this way that *fear is both the barrier to a full encounter with God and yet a necessary initiator and precursor of that experience*. The type of evil that visits punishment of an unremitting, intolerable and unjustified cruelty on an innocent victim is the outpouring of a deranged mind, or else one in psychic contact with demonic forces in the non-material world that can influence unduly sensitive people.

As one enters the realm of the other side of being, whose nature is negative and whose end is the annihilation of all personal identity, one experiences a fearful void in which all one's attributes and associations appear to be lost. It was by those that one had previously held fast to reality, and now they are dissipated. Punishment, especially if remorseless and unrelenting, tortures the body and humiliates the deeper personality. We feel degraded in the eyes of other people, and therefore retreat from those whom we had previously regarded as our friends. We first experience the fear of punishment when we are small, helpless little children. Small children identify themselves with their frail bodies and the intimate contact they enjoy in the company of those close to them in blood relationship or deep emotional sympathy. This contact is primarily psychical, but, of course, it must be acknowledged corporeally also, for we, as people, function not as disembodied spirits but as ensouled bodies infused by the Holy Spirit.

The fear that assails the psyche hovers like a heavy evening mist that envelops the landscape and obliterates the earthly landmarks in a pall of dark shapelessness. Indeed, intense fear can blot out our normal consciousness to the extent that we may later fail to remember the cause of the fear. This is a psychological defence mechanism that shields the psyche by occluding from it events of unbearable savagery with an intolerable emotional charge. But unfortunately this highly charged material does not remain dormant indefinitely; it mills around in the depths of the psyche, "the unconscious" as it is usually called, acting as the "enemy, the devil who, as a roaring lion, prowls around looking for someone to devour," whom we have already encountered in these pages. In the end it can cause so much emotional disturbance that, if not brought into the open and healed, it can lead to both mental breakdown and bodily disease.

The fear that vindictive punishment brings in its train is related not only to our own threatened well-being and safety but also to our sense of acceptance by other people. The person who is being humiliated is seldom an attractive associate for the worldly wise. Jesus knew this and warned His disciples of His coming trial and condemnation, and that they would flee away from Him in terror. In the more mundane circumstances of everyday life, we simply walk on the other side, as the priest and Levite did when they were confronted by the man who fell among thieves. We do not want to know, not only because the humiliated are a nuisance, demanding our time and attention, as in the case of the Parable of the Good Samaritan, but also because we may ourselves be associated with them in the minds of those important people whose worldly opinions we esteem. Poor Peter, in denying His Lord three times, clearly showed where his first loyalty lay — and few of us would fare better today. It is one thing to support victims of persecution verbally but at a safe distance — using them as a foil to beat a noisome political system with gestures. It is very different to harbour an escaped victim in one's own home, knowing that the reward for discovery would be ostracism by the community, severe punishment, and possibly death.

Fear of rejection is a terrible thing to bear. It is related to the fear of departure of those whom we love. The child knows these fears early in his life when those people with whom he had formed a warm and loving relationship move away from his orbit. This inevitable departure of people about their own business need not cause severe suffering if the child's parents and other close associates are affectionate and demonstrative in their love. But when, as sometimes happens, they are emotionally inadequate if not frankly uninterested in their offspring, the child experiences an unbearable sense of loss when someone who does seem to care suddenly goes out of his life. This is, in fact, a primitive experience of bereavement, but few attending adults would have the wit or sensitivity to appreciate the depth of the loss or of the inadequacy of substitutes. Relationships are all unique; a deep one cannot be perfunctorily replaced — indeed it is often irremediable, and a void is left to mark its memory. The experiences of rejection and the loss of someone for whom one cared deeply both reveal the essential emptiness of one's emotional life and point with frightening candour to the darkness that lies below the surface of frivolity and sociability that we present to the world. Indeed, this façade deceives no one more completely than the person who presents it. Our daily comfort depends almost entirely upon the way other people accept us — which in turn depends on the "image" we present to the world — and those few closer relationships that have an affectionate quality. When both are removed from us a terrible fear assails us, especially when we are small and not yet so mentally cultivated that we can lose ourselves in work and deliberation. The void left by the cessation of a deep relationship is like a bottomless pit that opens into the clear daylight of consciousness, but whose span embraces annihilation.

This is the ultimate fear, to be enveloped in such impenetrable darkness that one ceases to exist as a finite individual. Yet this apparent non-existence on a personal level is accompanied by a terror of the void that surrounds one. This is panic, and not a state of oblivion or unconsciousness. The awareness of annihilation crowns the fourfold terror of bodily destruction due to severe punishment, the humiliation of the ego that is a part of rejection by other people, the removal of the landmarks of intimate affection that follows the departure or death of the loved one in the experience of bereavement, and finally the total denial of the integrity of the person that can succeed events as separated in intensity as mere thought-lessness on the one hand or, on the other, brutal punishment in a prison camp where the tortures of the damned are suffered. In the state of annihilation of the ego, one can begin to understand what hell means and to glimpse the agony of Christ in Gethsemane. It is the most terrible experience that can befall any human being, and yet paradoxically, those who have undergone it are the most privileged of people. They alone are able to understand the full meaning of resurrection, for a great truth has been revealed to them concerning the nature of ultimate reality.

I began this exploration of fear by contrasting the negative, paralysing effect of fear and the positive, constructive value of prudence and providence. Fear in everyday life is to be deprecated. It shows itself in timidity and arrant cowardice. The genesis of this negative approach to life's adventure is an ill-starred experience of fear in one's earlier days. We should not try to escape the thrust of terror in our lives or the fear that this engenders. Those who do apparently escape this experience are to be pitied, not envied, for they are deprived of a true understanding of reality. Life remains for them superficially orientated, depending on continued happiness for its maintenance. But those who have experienced terror and fear must not be dominated by the encounter. These harrowing, yet essential, ingredients of life have to be integrated into the personality, after which they assume the positive aspects of prudence, providence, compassion and finally love.

Perfect love banishes fear (I John 4:18), but overwhelming fear must be experienced and accepted before perfect love may be known.

This is the path of life; it is the way of transfiguration.

Meditation

Whenever I experience fear, I identify myself with the weak and humble of the world. But may my sensitivity and vulnerability lead me to prayer and self-sacrifice on behalf of those less fortunate than I. As I give of myself to others, so paradoxically do I grow in strength until I can justly take my place among those who contend for the coming of the kingdom of God.

7

Psychic Darkness: the Collective Pain

The encounter with fear does not end on a purely personal plane; it has communal, indeed cosmic, overtones. In our private lives, we may think we are "windowless monads", to use a term from the philosophy of Leibnitz, but we can hardly stray from our own homes before we encounter other living forms. The homes to which I refer are not merely the places in which we dwell but are, much more significantly, our own minds. These are the "infinite hives" (to quote John Donne) in which are contained not only our private emotions and thoughts, but also a constant, yet ever changing, concourse of mental images from the world in which we live and the vast psychic sphere beyond rational consciousness. There are to be found the forms of minds that have passed beyond bodily death as well as those beings that have never been clothed in a physical body, the angelic intelligences and their demonic counterparts. This vast mass of intelligences, both benign and mischievous, are part of the mental world we inhabit.

To be unaware of this psychic milieu means that we cannot communicate in depth with our fellow human beings, because in our meaningful exchange of ideas it is usually what remains unsaid and undisclosed in sensory contact that contains the heart of the message. Although people are constantly subjecting themselves to a barrage of words that pass as conversation, they seldom actually listen to what they are saying, let alone to what the other person is feeling inwardly. Lao Tzu has wisely said: "Without stirring abroad one can know the whole world; without looking out of the window, one can see the way of heaven. The further one goes, the less one knows." This is the paradoxical logic of the mystic. He knows that his own being embraces the universe just as the universe embraces his own being. There is a psychic sympathy between the farthest star and the individual creature, however humble by human assessment, so that a cosmic harmony embraces all its parts. Jesus said likewise: "Are not sparrows two a penny? Yet without your Father's leave not one of them can fall to the ground. As for you, even the hairs of your head have all been counted. So have no fear; you are worth more than any number of sparrows" (Matthew 10:29–31).

This teaching of Christ illustrates both the indwelling nature of God in His creation, an insight especially dear to the mystical tradition, and the delineation of the creation into hierarchies of excellence, which brings in the vitally important consideration of moral values. Men are worth more than mere animals, not because the divine spark is limited to the human species, but because man, among all the animals of our world, has been given a rational mind and individual soul that can work in fellowship with God, as co-heir with Christ. To whom much is given, much is expected, and the responsibility inherent in the gifts can weigh heavily on the creature.

The psychic dimension is in constant interplay with our own souls, which though individual, are also in intimate communion with all other souls, and through the spirit with God. It is this spiritual communion with God and psychical interconnection with other souls that lies at the heart of intercessory prayer. This is not, as is sometimes rather naïvely thought, a willed telepathic interplay between two minds, that of the intercessor and that of the one being prayed for, so that a powerful personality can attempt to influence someone at a distance by extrasensory means. Such an attempt to influence another person would find its end in magic no matter how well-intentioned the motive. In true intercessory prayer, it is the Holy Spirit who links the person who prays with the one in need. The Holy Spirit interpenetrates the spirit of those who pray and knocks at the door of the soul of the one being prayed for. He does not effect a forced entry: the free will of each individual is sacrosanct and is not set on one side even by

God — He admittedly knocks at the door of the soul, but will not come in until He is made welcome. This is in great contrast to the work of the occultist who attempts to force the portals of another person's mind by telepathic communication. In the end that person would be in serious danger of enslavement to the practitioner of psychic power.

It can be seen from all that has been said, that the psychic realm is one of intimate communication by extrasensory means between various forms of intelligence. In itself it is morally neutral. Only when it is purified by the Spirit of God does it become a clear channel for spiritual communication. In its native form, however, it is sullied and darkened by perverse thoughts and negative attitudes that derive from maladjusted human beings and evil entities in the realm beyond death of the body. It is the inherent murkiness of the psychic dimension that has led to its being depreciated by most religious traditions. However, practitioners of these religions often fail to acknowledge that the prophetic or mystical impulse that inspired their founders and saints has come to them through the psychic realm; the same applies to the charismatic phenomena that are such a life-giving revelation to our present Christian scene.

Heraclitus says: "You can never find out the boundaries of the soul, so deep are they." The personality of man intermingles with all the psychic darkness that has accumulated from the misdeeds and vile thoughts of his forebears since the very dawn of his creation. It also has direct access to the ineffable Godhead through the vast communion of loved ones and their emergent energies in the realms beyond human exploration. The crown of this vast concourse is the God of rational theology (as opposed to mystical theology, if such a distinction is valid) who shows Himself to man as person to person, whose divine essences are known to Christians as Father, Son and Holy Spirit. In the Godhead the Holy Trinity finds its eternal generation, and "at the last day" even the Son will be made subordinate to God who made all things subject to Him, and thus God will be all in all (I Corinthians 15:28). The Trinity itself will be subsumed in the unity of the Godhead, and the creation story will have ended in the deification (the raising to the divine nature) of all things.

This vast cosmic plan of the raising of all things to God requires a preliminary identification of the higher nature with that which is low and debased. Thus it is that the Word of God, by whom all things are made, incarnates Himself fully in the form of a man (in our small planet) and takes on the burden of humanity. Though rejecting the temptation of setting Himself above anyone else, or, as would be said in theological terms, being without sin, He gives Himself voluntarily to take on the sin that has accumulated throughout the whole time of creation, in order to bear it even to the point of self-destruction. And in bearing it to the annihilation of His very reputation, so that He is numbered among the criminals, He redeems all that is sordid and disreputable and brings even this into the realm of the holy. This is the Christ story; it is the particular insight that the Christian religion has to offer mankind about the nature of reality shining as a faint yet inextinguishable light amid the gloom of the world's illusion.

The illusion has its own validity in our world, but it is empty of moral value and fails to satisfy the soul despite its attractiveness to the ignorant and unwise seeker. The darkness of this realm can easily irrupt into the consciousness of psychically sensitive people. Indeed, such sensitivity is a painful gift since it allows its possessor no rest; on the contrary, it makes him aware of the pain that afflicts the whole world. The wise of this world are well advised to avoid all knowledge of this sensitivity, since they can then remain restricted and enclosed in their small but cosy world of personal comfort. But those who are so obtuse in sensitivity as to escape contact with the darkness that pervades the psychic realm will not be able to relate fully with their fellows. The full openness of psychic sensitivity that leads one to enter the deepest recesses of hell is a terrible burden. But it brings with it, for those who can withstand the agony of the encounter, an ability to enter into the deepest experiences of other people and to act as agents of healing.

One does not plan an exploration of the negative force of the collective psychic hell. If one did, the ego would be in control, and through its lack of enlightenment the explorer would be led away from spiritual reality to a mere satisfaction of the innate desire that all men share for power over the natural order and the lives of other people. Far from planning an expedition into the dark psychic realm, one usually finds oneself there inadvertently and unwillingly in the course of one's work in the world. It seems that the aspiring person is gradually trained spiritually by the Holy Spirit to take on a greater burden of suffering as part of his service to the world. If he succeeds in this great enterprise, he emerges stronger and more fulfilled, and therefore able to take on more pain subsequently. The reward for service effectively carried out is more service; the end is the transfiguration of darkness to light, of evil to good. But when we are incarcerated in psychic gloom, this end is seldom tangible to us. Even Christ on the cross cried out in agony to His Father, Who appeared to have forsaken Him in His moment of greatest despair.

I have always believed that Jesus' greatest suffering was in the Garden of Gethsemane rather than the terrible six hours on the cross. The Gethsemane experience was interior and associated with the almost complete obliteration of the natural consciousness of a healthy man by overwhelming psychic darkness. Something of the intensity of this experience has been known by others also, though assuredly to a lesser degree, for no one other than the Word Made Flesh could have borne it on a human level and retained His sanity, indeed His life. The effect of being submerged in the darkness of the psychic realm — and here I do not refer particularly to demonic influences, but simply to the accumulated psychic debris of unredeemed sin that has found its expression in frank despair since the beginning of human consciousness and perhaps even further back than that — is a most terrible

depression. This depression is of such an intensity that it
obliterates all emotional response except overwhelming fear
of imminent annihilation. This is not the fear of death that we
all have to come to terms with in the course of our lives on
earth. The worst — and some people would say the best —
that this threat of personal obliteration can bring is a sense of
total oblivion such as occurs in a deep, dreamless sleep. To the
unbeliever death is comparable to a state of sleep or general
anaesthesia, such as is induced before a surgical operation,
with the crucial difference that there is to be no awakening.
Those whose lives have for one reason or another been hellish
cannot be blamed for welcoming the possibility of total personal annihilation; indeed such a view, unsatisfactory as it is in
achieving a full understanding of growth of the person in the
knowledge of God, is no less unworthy than one that sees
survival of death in terms of personal comfort for services
rendered to God. Until the ego is displaced from the customary
seat of pre-eminence, it will dominate our views about survival.
The ego looks for rewards, the soul seeks eternal life in God.
The difference between these two approaches to reality is vast.

I have often heard it asserted that Jesus' agony in the
garden was due to the sudden realisation of His impending
death. It is hard to believe that such a mighty soul would flinch
from this natural event in the lives of all creatures with this
degree of dread. He above all others had little to fear on a
personal level, so blameless had His life been. I find it much
more probable that, in Gethsemane, the burden of the psychic
load of sin incurred by the cosmos was laid on His own person,
and the despair that this engendered brought Him to the
breaking-point of His own mental stability. It is recorded in
the Synoptic Gospels how anguish and grief came over Him,
and He said that His heart was ready to break with grief.
He fell on His face in prayer and begged His Father to let
the cup pass Him by, but nevertheless according to God's
will, not His own. This agony was repeated twice more; the
disciples slept (which means that they were simply not with

their master since their field of consciousness was so limited), and Jesus was enveloped in the dark, acrid stench of psychic hell, which, not without reason, has been compared with sulphurous fumes. These fumes penetrate the whole person, affecting the physical body with a sense of having the heart torn out of the chest and the throat so constricted that breathing becomes painful. The desire to vomit is almost uncontrollable. The darkness of hell has the final effect of dismembering the whole psyche. If left unimpeded, it would kill the body and smash the soul so that the creature would be returned void to the primal chaos whence it had been fashioned.

All this Jesus experienced completely alone. The ultimate temptation of His ministry was to fail, under its terrible impact, and in the words of Job's wife, to curse God and die. But He persisted. The key to His triumph in this darkest of moments lay in His rapt prayer to God. He was able to lift Himself up — or perhaps it would be more appropriate to say that He allowed Himself to be lifted up in prayer — to God, through the acrid fumes of psychic despair. This is one of the greatest fruits of prayer. In Luke's account of the agony (22:39–46), it is stated that an angel appeared from heaven bringing Him strength, and in anguish of spirit He prayed the more urgently, and His sweat was like clots of blood falling to the ground. However we interpret this angelic presence (I personally accept it literally), the episode tells us that in spontaneous "arrow" prayer of rapt intensity, one can be available to the whole company of heaven who will sustain one in one's most agonised moments. But the cup is not removed — it never is in the hard school of life — and every drop of the bitter potion has to be drained to the dregs. Yet somehow this forbidding task becomes easier as the draught is swallowed. Even the darkness of hell can become tolerable when one has had the courage to persist in faith. But this faith is a gift of the Holy Spirit, and it is attained by the practice of intensive prayer and self-giving to God and man. For those who do not have this burning intensity of faith, the temptation to cut short their lives can be almost irresistible.

The one who has tasted the dregs of psychic despair and inhaled the acrid fumes that spell death to all mortal passion, and yet has survived the ordeal, emerges as a changed person. It is as if he were born again; he has passed through the dominion of death and come out alive on the other side. "When anyone is united to Christ, there is a new world; the old order is gone, and a new order has already begun" (II Corinthians 5:17). This well-known account of the new life in Christ that St Paul described is especially true of the person who has had the courage and the faith to hold on to God through the ultimate baptismal experience, the experience of which Jesus Himself had to partake fully before He was ready for resurrection. When Jesus tells Nicodemus that a man has to be born over again before he can see the kingdom of God (John 3:3), He may well be pointing to this ultimate experience, for all earlier encounters with the Holy Spirit are as introductions to the mystical life compared with this cataclysmic initiation into the reality of darkness and its ultimate transmutation to the light. The great change that marks this final initiation is the capacity for full, universal love. We will return to this topic later.

But there are, I believe, many people who have felt the impress of only a small degree of psychic darkness and have not been able to bear it. These may be among those individuals who have been driven to putting an end to their own mortal lives. When a person, in the depths of an overwhelming depression, attempts suicide, it is, in my opinion, an excruciating experience of inner dereliction and disintegration that drives him to this extreme act of self-destruction. It has been shown me that people seldom take their own lives as an intellectual protest against the insoluble difficulties inherent in existence. It is much more likely that the act of committing suicide is a way of escape from the intolerable darkness that obfuscates the personality of the one under trial. Of course, like all categorical assertions, this too has its exceptions and modifications; it may well be that there are some mentally-polarised pessimists who view the world quite dispassionately as a vale of fruitless suffering, and whose nihilistic philosophy leads them to opt out of life quite deliberately. However, this type of cerebral detachment is not the way of real living people whose existence is intimately bound up with the flow of the universe.

The little ones of God live courageously a day at a time, knowing intuitively that they are provided for moment by moment even when the future appears hopeless and the present is scarcely bearable. But when psychic darkness descends on them, even this innate confidence in the providence of God is obliterated and they have the experience of drowning in a vast sea of dark, meaningless chaos. It is probably this experience that induces the victims of severe depression to end their lives. Who could blame them for resorting to this extreme action? Yet, if they were able to withstand the temptation to quit this life, and instead persist in the name of God who seems to have hidden Himself completely from them, they would, quite literally, be saved. The greatest privilege that lies in store for the person who has emerged from the valley of the shadow of death is the ability to guide his brethren through that same valley to the delectable mountains that lie beyond it.

I have in this account touched on what I regard as the most terrible suffering that can befall a human being: the total obliteration of all hope in an ocean of psychic darkness that finds the victim drawn into the chaos of non-existence from which we are told the world was created (II Maccabees 7:28). And yet in that non-existence, the awareness of self persists. This paradox resembles that of the directly opposite experience of mystical union with God. In this supreme illumination, the ego is obliterated in the uncreated light of the Godhead, and yet for the first time in his life the mystic experiences his true being. As St Paul puts it, "The first man,

Adam, became an animate being whereas the last Adam has become a life-giving spirit" (I Corinthians 15:45).

It was no chance event that Christ's transfiguration preceded His agony and His descent into hell. No doubt the spiritual illumination of the great mystical experience of eternity helped Him in the journey into darkness that punctuated the final period of His ministry.

Meditation

Though my life has, up until this moment, apparently been one of ease and fulfilment, may I never be far in thought and prayer from those who are overwhelmed by the sin of the world. I too can be a soldier of Christ when I remember Him in steadfast love by praying without ceasing for the coming of the kingdom. This I do by keeping the name of God in my remembrance at all times no matter how trivial the work at hand. Whatever I do with my whole heart directed to God plays its part in lightening the burden of the world. And when I may be called on to suffer, I too will be sustained.

8

The Heart of Suffering

The encounter with psychic despair and disintegration is the ultimate trial in the life of one who is destined to know God and be transformed into His image. Only he who has confronted the darkest depth of himself — and therefore of the whole created universe, so close is the solidarity between the person and the cosmos — can bring that unfathomed hell to God, Who will redeem it through the mediation of His Son, for He took on the form of the most despised criminal in order to save the world. He who flinches from the ultimate darkness flinches also from a true knowledge of God. To worship God in the light of His glory and His love is within the bounds of even a sinful man. To worship God in His impenetrable obscurity is the vocation of a saint — and we are all destined to become sanctified human beings. "I am the Lord, there is no other; I make the light and create darkness, author alike of prosperity and trouble. I, the Lord, do all these things" (Isaiah 45:6–7). In a subsequent passage we read: "Surely God is among you, and there is no other, no other God. How then canst thou be a god that hidest thyself, O God of Israel, the deliverer?" (Isaiah 45:14–15). God appears to hide Himself from us when things are going wrong, at least by our understanding of fortune and misfortune, but until we can know the divine presence in the darkness of unknowing as clearly as in the light of reason, the one we know is not God.

The knowledge of God of which I speak, is an intense, glowing inner relationship, the authenticity of which is proved by our change from the separative human consciousness of everyday life to the unitive participation in eternal values. It is the same knowledge that the blessed spouses of antiquity had of each other when a child of promise was conceived: Abraham and Sarah, Elkanah and Hannah, Zechariah and Elizabeth. Isaac, Samuel and John the Baptist were the fruit of this inner knowledge, of whom the Holy Spirit is the true mediator. And all culminates in the fully virginal conception of Jesus Christ, which is a mystery to be withheld from the gaze of the uncomprehending until the end of time. Only then will the glory of a full birth in God be revealed for all to understand. When one can worship God in the stillness of obscurity as well as in the light of His manifest presence, one has attained a level of prayer that can never cease, but proceeds from glory to glory until all that is created is carried up into the throne where the angels cry perpetually: "Holy, holy, holy is the Lord of Hosts; the whole earth is full of His glory."

The encounter with God's obscurity need not always be mediated by mental or emotional torment. Our physical body, the body of our humiliation which is sown in the innocence of childhood and flourishes in the glory of youth, is also the scene of our ageing and decay. To the chagrin of those practitioners of the occult who are dominated by the gnostic view of reality that matter is evil (if not illusory) and spirit alone is good and real, the physical body does make its claims on our attention and its demands on our solicitude. These esotericists tell us to get beyond the body, to rise above its discomforts and enter the purely spiritual world of elevated thought and rapt contemplation. It is fortunate for us lesser mortals that the divine nature did not spurn the virgin's womb, nor consider it beneath His dignity to assume human flesh and bone and live amongst us as an ordinary man. It is, in fact, impossible to ignore the claims of the body since it is the temple of the Holy Spirit while we are alive in this world, and it is the means of our activity in whatever situation we find ourselves. It is also destined to be resurrected to full spirituality according to the resurrection shown by the humiliated body of Jesus; indeed, the way of authentic spirituality is through our body of flesh to the Word of God who dwelt in a similar body. The way of ascent that tries to evade the encumbrance of that body leads to the void of unreality, not the vale of divinity. There are not a few of us who will attain a knowledge of eternal values through the agency of the physical body, not so much in its glorious moments of joy and prowess as in the longer period of decline and dissolution.

The body is the seat of much personal anguish. It is not only the receptacle of pain in its many forms, but it also registers that failure in function that makes life so tragic, especially during the last period of earthly existence. How much do we take the faculties of sight and hearing for granted when all is going well! How seldom do we thank God that our digestive and excretory functions are working smoothly until illness strikes! If we were living in full command of the moment, we would be aware of every incident that occurred around us and would thank our Creator for every healthy impulse we felt within ourselves. The practice of awareness is an essential exercise in spiritual development. We will never reach a comprehension of divine things while we remain unmoved by earthly things. "If a man says 'I Love God', while hating his brother, he is a liar. If he does not love the brother whom he has seen, it cannot be that he loves God whom he has not seen" (I John 4:19). This statement of the way of love reminds us that we work from the known to the unknown. In the end we discover that it is through a perfect knowledge of the known, that which we take casually for granted day after day, that we discover the unknown within it. The glory of God, His Spirit that pervades all created things, is found in the little things of life, those which we often dismiss summarily as being of no value or a waste of time.

As we become proficient through experience in the knowledge of earthly things, so our bodies begin to fail us and we find ourselves confronted by such misfortunes as a progressive failure of sight or hearing. To an extent this curtailment of our means of external communication with those around us is an inevitable accompaniment of growing old, though I have little doubt that people who love their bodies and cherish their faculties tend to enjoy a physical usefulness even at an advanced age. Conversely, those who squander their physical resources in selfish indulgence tend to reap the fruits of their folly in a premature failure of vital bodily function. This is not, of course, the whole story. Some people appear to thrive on a riotous, hedonistic way of life whereas others, of apparently blameless disposition, are marked out for progressive crippling diseases even in their youth. The end of individual life is inscrutable to human understanding, as the prophets and sages of Israel knew when they debated these deep matters in their own hearts with God. "O Lord, I will dispute with thee, for thou art just: yes, I will plead my case before thee. Why do the wicked prosper and traitors live at ease? Thou hast planted them and their roots strike deep, they grow up and bear fruit. Thou art ever on their lips, yet far from their hearts. But thou knowest me, O Lord, thou seest me; thou dost test my devotion to thyself" (Jeremiah 12:1–2). The tragedy of human suffering lies not only in the terrible agony of pain, impotence and despair, but even more in the obvious trans-gression of the law of justice in the individual life that all men cherish no matter how often they betray it in their behaviour.

The answer to Jeremiah's question about the manifest in-equality of men's destiny according to their deserts was given to some extent in the subsequent history of Israel: most of the people were exterminated, but a chosen, chastened remnant returned from Babylonian exile to recolonise the Holy Land. But were all those who did not return from exile evil men? Were they all less worthy than the survivors? Amongst those who died miserably in Egypt, and through no fault of his own, was Jeremiah himself. His confessions record a constant dialogue of revolt against the unfathomable will of God, and God no more explains His ways to Jeremiah than He does to the fictitious Job. In that masterpiece of religious literature, Job has to confront the mystery of a transcendent God who has created all things according to His will. In the great Hindu scripture, the *Bhagavadgita*, the warrior Arjuna is in constant conversation with the incarnate lord Krishna, who again tells him to get on with his duty as a warrior and to redress evil actions with the sword. In the Eastern scriptures the fact of survival of death and a rebirth sequence into new phases of life is taken for granted — a view that appears to have some substantiation according to recent psychical studies — so that the manifest unfairness and tragedy of this life is painted on a vaster canvas of time. But Arjuna too is shown the terrible side of God, so that he flinches in awe and is brought to silence. "Time am I, world-destroying, grown mature, engaged here in subduing the world. Even without thy action, all the warriors standing arrayed in the opposing armies shall cease to be" (*Bhagavadgita*, 11:32).

The body is our instrument of self-expression when we are young and vigorous. As we become older and decrepit, so it becomes our prison of isolation. The prospect of old age, especially when accompanied by disease and immobility, is forbidding to all of us, but especially to the sensualist. No longer can he escape the reality of the present moment by magnificent exploits into personal grandeur, for he is increasingly anchored to an inefficient, failing mechanism that thwarts his every action. The diseased, ageing body is a tomb in which the truth of its occupant's life is recorded day by day. Its suffering is the moment of truth continually revealed to the person, and its end marks the completion of one portion of the individual's life. To grow in spirit while incarcerated in a failing body is to make use of the present misfortune for eternal blessing. Just as the person who has traversed the gloom of psychic despair and emerged on the other side as a changed being radiates the light of God, so the sufferer who has moved beyond the imprisonment of an irremediably failing body to spiritual understanding is an agent of healing for the world. The great truth of Isaiah 53:5 is borne in on us: "By his scourging we are healed"; indeed, we shall have to investigate this doctrine further, for on it depends the healing ministry of pain. The one who has experienced this crucial ministry in his own life can alone be an effective agent of God's healing powers.

The problem of personal suffering is not finally solved until we move beyond the emotional limitations of an ego-centred consciousness. All attempts at justifying the ways of God — indeed a belief in the very existence of a divine agency in the face of the world's unrelieved suffering — fail, in the end, to convince any save those who already believe on deeper spiritual grounds. The exercise of theodicy moves uncomfortably between the Scylla of a loving God unable to control the world He has fashioned and the Charybdis of an omnipotent God whose ways are not those of the creatures He has made and who cares at most only peripherally about their well-being. In other words, there appears to be a limit either to His power or to His love. Jesus reminded His disciples that the Galileans whose blood Pilate had mixed with their sacrifices were no more sinful than their compatriots who were left unharmed. Likewise, the eighteen people who perished under the collapsed tower of Siloam were no more guilty than all the other people living in Jerusalem. But those who were left behind had a chance of repenting lest a similar type of disaster should befall them also (Luke 13:1–5).

The arbitrary nature of God's actions is so disturbing to our sense of justice that even God's friends seek hard to make Him obey the rule in their hearts. Did not Abraham say to God, "Shall not the judge of all the earth do what is just?" (Genesis 18:25). In this episode God agreed to spare the cities of Sodom and Gomorrah if even ten just men could be found in them. As human conscience grows in understanding, so the suffering servant, made manifest in Jesus, can give up his life for the redemption of the world. But the justice of this is overshadowed by the love revealed in unremitting self-sacrifice. To the unbeliever the arbitrary workings of fate present less of a problem; he simply denies the existence of a divine agency, and attributes human bestiality and natural disasters, such as Jesus discussed, to the deranged workings of the human mind and the impersonal forces of nature. In this respect we accept the natural powers without comment when all goes well for us, but do not cease to complain when these same powers turn against our interests and threaten to put an end to human life.

But there is a yearning for a morally perfect world deep in our hearts; it is the outer manifestation of the immanent God in every soul, who reveals Himself in the human spirit. It is apparent that there is no rational explanation for the fact of evil in the presence of a loving, all-powerful God. Even if we attempt to explain a present misfortune on the basis of a bad action performed in a previous existence — an approach that satisfies most adherents of the hypothesis of rebirth — we are in no way nearer understanding the origin of that bad action than we are the present misfortune that may have accrued from it. The expedient of time, whether in the past or towards the future, extends our present suffering on a wider scale, but it neither explains its origins nor points to its solution. This incidentally is why those pictures of the afterlife that promise personal rewards based on our present attitudes and actions fail to impress the truly spiritual soul. "Plus ça change, plus c'est la même chose" is the real objection of authentic spirituality both to the welfare-state type of humanism that dominates our worldly aspirations and the ego-centred spiritualism that many people associate with the life beyond death. While, of course, we should all work towards the relief of injustice, suffering and poverty wherever we find them, we should also begin to realise that the agencies of reason that dominate our lives on earth are poor instruments for this work of social healing. Only a complete inner change will suffice and this is not to be effected by human manipulations. It comes from the Spirit of God to those who are open to the healing power of suffering. These, needless to say, are the few, the very few, but they form the company of saints and martyrs on whom the welfare of the world depends. But their number is not restricted, as is the case with human societies that exclude all except an elect membership; rather it is we who exclude ourselves from this truly elect brotherhood by refusing to take up our cross in faith and come with our Master.

Most people gauge their usefulness to society by the intensity of their activities. Most people judge the success of their lives by their capacity to accumulate things, whether these be money, friends or power. The meaning of their life is dependent on what they can acquire; indeed the material commodities of this world are amongst the most innocuous, since their life history is limited. The acquisitions based on power and influence are far more dangerous since their effects can long outlast the life of their progenitor. But there comes a time when we can no longer be of use in the way that we would have it, when the acquisitions on which our sense of belonging depends are taken from us, and when we have to face our essential nakedness. This stark truth is usually borne in on us through the inroads of incurable disease or else the inevitable process of growing old. As the Buddha was shown at the beginning of his ministry — as I have already mentioned — the three final facts of mortal life are ageing, disease and death. They each immobilise us and bring us to confront our impotence as living beings. A fourth tragedy that has come to the forefront in our allegedly civilised century is the unjust imprisonment of many people for prolonged periods of time on account of their religion, race or political opinions.

When a person is confronted with the fact of his powerlessness in the face of ill-health or indefinite imprisonment, he undergoes different phases of response. There is first his childish incredulity that anything so final and irrevocable could happen to him. Of course we all know that these things are to be, but they are for others only, never for ourselves, because we are in some way special. Indeed, each one of us is special in his own way, but the uniqueness of that person lies in his particular contribution to the whole and not in his exemption from suffering. Indeed, the Lord told the Israelites: "For you alone have I cared among all the nations of the world; therefore will I punish you for all your iniquities" (Amos 3:2). In this instance the terrible sufferings that Amos was the first of the writing prophets to predict were the result of apostasy and idolatry. But later on in the career of the Jews, suffering takes on a different character in the person of the suffering servant described in Isaiah 53. Clearly a new way of life is opening for the sufferer, the end of which is stili beyond his imagination.

When the reality of the new situation has been fully grasped, the sufferer tries to wriggle out of it by devious routes. Once orthodox medicine has proved unavailing, recourse is had to a host of alternative therapies including what is called spiritual healing from various agencies, ranging from the charismatic to the spiritualistic. Each in turn may provoke an amelioration, but in due course there is a return to progressive enfeeblement, and the false hope of esoteric teachings is followed by the despair grounded in reality. Likewise those suffering prolonged, unjust imprisonment may delude themselves with hopes of early release because of their special connections with those in authority. Some may even collaborate with their persecutors in order to curry favour and attain freedom. But there comes, in due course, the final realisation that the process is irreversible. One can go on, but there is no turning back. This is the moment of truth; at last the victim has arrived at adult stature. "No one who sets his hand to the plough and then keeps looking back is fit for the kingdom of God" (Luke 9:62). Admittedly the sufferer would protest that he is not aiming at the celestial kingdom but aspiring only to the health or freedom that he once enjoyed. But in fact he is on the journey to a new dimension of reality, whether he accepts it or not. Like Job, he is in the hands of the powers that destroy, and none of his protests can arrest the process. He can either quit the race on a suicidal note or else persist against all odds.

When the fact of suffering's irreversibility has been finally grasped, there is a period of revolt. The previously religious man's faith in God is severely taxed — indeed the ritual superstition that so often passes for true religion will soon be abandoned. This so-called faith is really a travesty of true spirituality; it is more like a spiritual insurance policy against the day of trouble than the way of transforming the ego-consciousness into something resembling a real person. Even Job's obsequious religious observances aimed at placating a jealous God whom his hedonistic children might have offended, came to an abrupt end when misfortune struck him and reduced him to a pauper with a repulsive skin disease, sitting down in an ash-heap. The stricken Job contends with God, refusing to submit gratuitiously when he knows his own conscience is unclouded. For the first time in his life he has begun to relate to God, not in rapt awe, but in personal dispute. There are indeed many passionate atheists, passionate because of the manifest wrongs in our world, who are much closer to the God they deny than those religious devotees and fanatics who spend their time worshipping God and defending Him against heresy and unbelief. The atheist is in conversation with a real being, while the devotee is more often in fact worshipping a mental construction that assumes the power of an idol. If he knew God authentically, he would be at peace with himself and the world.

The religious person has to come to terms with the un-palatable fact that God is at the centre of the trouble. He was as much involved in the extermination of European Jewry by the Nazis in our own time as He was in the destruction of the Temple in Jerusalem and the exile of His people in 587 BC. These terrible thoughts, so often averted from the gaze of the pious during smooth times of peace and affluence, come to us like burning darts at the moment of calamity. We who think we can fathom the divine mind stand speechless before the terrible power of God's Word. "Where can I escape from thy spirit? Where can I flee from thy presence? If I climb up to heaven, thou art there; if I make my bed in Sheol, again I find thee . . . If I say 'Surely darkness will steal over me, night will close round me', darkness is no darkness for thee and night is luminous as day; to thee both dark and light are one" (Psalm 139:7–12). It is the same Lord who appeared to Moses in the burning bush and gave him his commission to lead the Jews out of Egyptian captivity that met Moses in the night, while they were encamped, meaning to kill him (Exodus 4:24–26). Only the action of his wife Zipporah, in performing an immediate circumcision, caused God to let Moses alone. To the modern mind this story is repulsive and hideously primitive, but it nevertheless is an episode of initiation comparable with the conflict between Jacob and the angel of God, again occurring during the night. The act of circumcision identified Moses, who had had a privileged position in Pharoah's court, categorically with the Jews whom he had been commissioned to save from destruction.

The sufferer has to learn that the justice of man is but a pale image of the providence of God. The divine way is not to maintain the *status quo* or even to initiate a movement to reform. There has to be a new insight which finds its consummation in a completely changed person. Thus all that Job had secretly feared had to come upon him before he could be so transformed as to bear the vision of the living God and hear the story of continuous creation. In the vision of God's transcendent majesty, Job's suffering took on the severity of a child's complaint. This is the end of personal suffering — to prove oneself worthy of it. For it is the supreme fulfilment of becoming fully human — and therefore starting to partake fully of the divine nature to which we were all called at the moment of our creation.

Only when one has come to this great transformation can one begin to fathom the ineffable glory of God, whom the greatest mystics have told us is beyond good and evil. In Him, what we call the power of good and evil are both eternally transformed. In the Spirit they issue forth as life, the life abundant which is eternal. No wonder Jesus Himself refused to be called good when the rich young man asked Him what he had to do to win eternal life (Mark 10:18). Though He was supremely good by human standards, yet Jesus knew that in His carnal body He could not transcend the polarities of good and evil. This experience was to be His only in the final part of His ministry, starting most horribly in the Garden of Gethsemane and ending triumphantly, by way of the cross and the descent into hell, at the moment of bodily resurrection.

Meditation

Grant me the strength, O Lord, so to traverse the valley of death's shadow that I may emerge from the other side a better, more compassionate person of greater use to you as a witness and to my brothers as a servant.

9

Strength in Weakness

What then is this change that God has decreed for the real person? It is to replace the purely human nature with that which is divine, or better still, to put the divine body over the physical edifice that we now inhabit.

"No wonder we do not lose heart! Though our outward humanity is in decay, yet day by day we are inwardly renewed. Our troubles are slight and short-lived; and their outcome an eternal glory which outweighs them far. Meanwhile our eyes are fixed, not on the things that are seen, but on the things that are unseen: for what is seen passes away; what is unseen is eternal. For we know that if the earthly frame that houses us today should be demolished, we possess a building which God has provided — a house not made of human hands, eternal, and in heaven. In this present body we do indeed groan; we yearn to have our heavenly habitation put on over this one — in the hope that, being thus clothed, we shall not find ourselves naked. We groan indeed, we who are enclosed within this earthly frame; we are oppressed because we do not want to have the old body stripped off. Rather our desire is to have the new body put on over it, so that our mortal part may be absorbed into life immortal. God Himself has shaped us for this very end; and as a pledge of it He has given us the Spirit" (II Corinthians 4:16–5:5).

In this remarkable passage St Paul reaches one of his greatest mystical peaks. He has, in a heavenly vision, glimpsed and charted the whole course of human evolution from the purely animal nature to the resplendent effulgence of spiritual transfiguration. And yet this humble nature in which we groan in the pangs of perpetual suffering is not simply to be discarded as a worn-out piece of clothing fit only for the rubbish heap. It is to be changed by the imposition of the Spirit of God so that it enjoys a complete resurrection to eternal life.

This vision sharply distinguishes between the predestined immortality of the soul, which is a measure of God's love for all He has created, and the raising up of the material universe from corruption to splendour, which is the meaning of the resurrection of the body. For this resurrection to take place, there is full collaboration between the Creator and His creatures, notably the human being in our little planet. The Mediator of this divine-human covenant is the Word Made Flesh who dwelt among us, and demonstrated this bodily resurrection when He groaned pitifully under the accumulated suffering of all creation.

This change from the purely personal human mode to the transpersonal mode of the aspirant for God is a gradual process. It may manifest itself assuredly in sudden spurts of renewed spiritual grace and inner illumination, but these tend to be episodes of ecstasy that punctuate spiritual development rather than typify it. The change is essentially an inward one, and its fruits are initially more evident to the outside observer than to the person himself. Indeed, if one believes that one is making constant spiritual progress and especially if one talks confidently about it and boasts about one's developing spiritual gifts to others, there is every probability that one is being directed along an aberrant psychic pathway which leads not to the vision of God, but to ego-centred delusion and stultification. The change that is real concerns the deflection of the personal will from self-gratification to a greater participation in the life of the community and the knowledge of God. In other words the ego is shifted from its accustomed seat of authority in the world of man to its cloister of service in God's Kingdom, whose ruler is the Holy Spirit and whose place of operation in the human personality is the apex of the soul.

In the life of suffering the essential change that occurs in the personality of the one who is growing under its hard tutelage is a shift from egocentricity to charity. Whereas previously the centre of awareness of the sufferer was firmly based on himself, he himself making the complaints to God and demanding an explanation in the manner of Job among his comforters, he now starts to see that the real life is one focussed on God and his own existence has to be subordinated to God's will. Whereas earlier he felt he knew God's will in terms of scriptural authority appropriately interpreted to fit in with his own view of life, now he does not attempt to define the deep things of life in terms of human reason. Instead he realises that the beatific vision consists in a perfect relationship between himself and God — Who is best defined as "He who is" — in which subject and object are transformed beyond the polarities of discursive thought to the unity of identity in love. "By love may he be gotten and holden, but by thought never" says the anonymous author of *The Cloud of Unknowing*. It is through the transformation wrought by intense suffering — on the few, the very few, it must be insisted — that universal love takes the place of those constant demands for personal satisfaction that mark the way of the unenlightened person.

In the great theophany that forms the summit of the saga of Job's afflictions, God reveals His magnificence as the eternal creator who is ceaselessly making all things new, but He gives no account of the inner workings of the divine mind nor does He explain the deeper springs of Job's terrible suffering. And Job would have no interest in having the heavenly wager between the light and darkness of God's providence explained to him. He has passed beyond the polarities of good and evil, light and darkness, happiness and suffering, to the ultimate realm in which the being of God is the only reality. When Job says at the vision of God's revelation of Himself: "I know that thou canst do all things and that no purpose is beyond thee. But I have spoken of great things which I have not understood, things too wonderful for me to know. I knew of thee then only by report but now I see thee with my own eyes. Therefore I melt away, I repent in dust and ashes" (Job 42:2–6), he has learned the full lesson of his suffering. The "I" that was the

authentic Job, worthy of eternity, has become established in
the vision that God vouchsafed to Job. This true self transforms
the whole personality into something of the nature of God.
Thus it is said: "The first man, Adam, became an animate
being, whereas the last Adam has become a life-giving spirit"
(I Corinthians 15:45). Indeed, I am convinced that St Irenaeus
was inspired by eternal wisdom when he saw that all human
life was to be a recapitulation of the life of Christ, both in this
world and in the greater world that lies beyond the veil that we
call death.

This change of attitude from regarding life as a possession
and a right to one of being joyously thankful for the privilege
of participating in it, comes slowly in the understanding of any
one individual. We are schooled in the belief that the measure
of successful living is the attainment of definite ends: a place
of esteem among our fellows, material possessions and a
respectable income, a family responsibility which we parade
proudly to the world and in which we can find inner security
and repose, a means of employment by which we can affirm
ourselves. None of these requirements is contemptible, nor
to be disregarded. But they are all subordinate to something
even more needful for immediate salvation and eternal hope;
a fixed centre within oneself that radiates the fire of God,
which in turn integrates the personality and leads one on to
mental and bodily health. Even on a purely material level the
first requirement for a satisfactory life is a healthy body; all the
money that the world is able to offer can in no way compensate
for defective sight or hearing, a painful, inefficient limb, or
the inability to breathe comfortably. It is only when we are
checked by some bodily infirmity that we begin to realise how
dependent we are on the humble physical mechanism that we
take shamefully for granted day after day. We can now fully
articulate the praise of the Psalmist: "When I look up at thy
heavens, the work of thy fingers, the moon and the stars set in
their place by thee, what is man that thou shouldst remember
him, mortal man that thou shouldst care for him? Yet thou

hast made him little less than a god, crowning him with glory and honour" (Psalm 8:3–5).

Man's destiny is indeed to partake fully of the divine nature, but this means putting away the superficial logic and expectations of the humanistic man-god and taking on the humility and suffering of the God-man who came to raise the world from suffering to eternal life. Suffering starts by bringing us to see ourselves clearly in our present situation and showing us what we may become in the life of eternity. Suffering ends when we and the whole creation have been lifted up from the illusory world of separation and division to the unity of the divine nature whose essence is love.

This statement is not to be seen merely as a sermon on the meaning and end of suffering, such as might be delivered by an impassioned preacher. It reflects rather something that suddenly comes to the aware sufferer at the zenith of his agony when he can contend no more with the "slings and arrows of outrageous fortune", when he comes to his breaking-point. He can either give up the apparently unequal struggle and quit this mortal life, or else he can remain in control of himself and continue to wrestle with a "sea of troubles" as Jacob wrestled with the angel of the Lord in the pitch-black obscurity of the long night. Only then does the blessing come — his name is changed, which means that his fundamental nature is transformed. Just as Jacob is renamed Israel, which means God strove, because Jacob strove with God and with men and prevailed (Genesis 32:28), so the sufferer who has passed beyond mortal breaking-point and still maintains his integrity emerges with a changed perspective on life. The things he previously regarded as of cardinal importance, such as affluence, the opinions of other people, material success and intellectual certainty, now fade into the background. They are seen to be childish illusions, mere idols of the mind. Instead the triumphant sufferer knows a peace that passes all understanding. He has, without fully realising it, moved from the death that we mistakenly call life to the

only real life, which is the eternity of love in God. Would it be
so strange if what we call this mortal life were really only a
dream and its awakening the moment of bodily death! The
peaks of suffering and the ecstasy that accrues from it make
this inverted vision of reality the ultimate truth. But we must
be worthy of this vision.

Peace is not a state of perpetual immobility or inertia in
which nothing more need ever happen. It is a relationship of
intimate communion with God, and it manifests itself outwardly in harmonious activity in whatever situation the person
finds himself. This ranges from the cosmic harmony known to
the greatest mystics to the workaday co-operation between
two simple souls in the common round of earthly life. Peace is
the strength that is given to the weak who have accepted their
present impotence and are not ashamed to give themselves, in
their apparent uselessness, to God. Thus it comes about that
intense suffering is the most powerful stimulus to confession,
and the inevitable way to absolution and healing. When the
tax-gatherer gives himself unreservedly to God in his worthless
sinfulness, he goes home acquitted of his sins. The Pharisee,
by contrast, though much more worthy in the world's eyes,
has seen his good works as a means of separating himself from
his less acceptable brethren. His good works have in fact been
performed without charity. He is still ego-centred, and believes
that his works justify him in God's esteem. There can in fact
be only one valid end in performing any good work — that of
offering it as a pure gift to God and one's fellow men. The
impulse is unconditional love. All alleged good works that
feed the ego of the person who performs them turn sour and
are a stumbling-block both to that person and to others who
are expected to benefit from them. It is noteworthy that two
essentially similar works may have diametrically opposed
results. One, performed in the disinterestedness of universal
love, will transform the consciousness of those who benefit
from the action. The other, performed with the ulterior motive
of self-justification, merely separates the agent from his

brethren and brings in its train the fruits of condescension, division and resentment. It is not surprising that some types of well-intentioned social activities, based on purely rational grounds, fail to produce happiness or satisfaction among those whom they are designed to help. We dare not set ourselves above even the meanest of our brethren, for we are all one in the vision of God. The mighty shall be abased and the humble exalted. Suffering brings this great truth down from the realm of thought to the heart of life. Its apogee is the cross on which the Lord of Life was killed in the company of two criminals with whom He identified Himself unconditionally.

The contemporary existentialist psychotherapist, Viktor Frankl, has written what is for me the most significant book about suffering in our century. His book, *Man's Search for Meaning*, describes his own experience as a Jewish doctor in various Nazi concentration camps, and he writes about suffering, as indeed do those few who write authentically about this harrowing subject, from the inside, having traversed the pit of hell and emerged bereft yet entire. He found that those who survived this most terrible of all experiences, terrible both by virtue of the unparalleled cruelty visited on the prisoners and the vicious injustice of their indictment, owed their preservation to the inner meaning that they found in their lives. He quotes Nietzsche's words: "He who has a *why* to live for can bear almost any *how*." He also quotes Dostoievsky: "There is only one thing I dread: not to be worthy of my sufferings." He describes the moving instance of a young woman who was dying in a concentration camp. She was cheerful in spite of a clear knowledge of her impending death. She said she was grateful that fate had hit her so hard because previously she had been spoiled and had not taken spiritual accomplishments seriously. She said that now the only friend she had in her loneliness was a tree that she could see outside the window of her hut. She often spoke to this tree. When Frankl asked her, thinking that she was suffering from hallucinations on account of her mortal sickness, if the tree replied, she said: "Yes, it said to me, 'I am here — I am life, eternal life.' "

It must be admitted in clear realism that the heroes and martyrs of prison camps form a spiritual elite. The majority of us, lesser mortals, would behave as Jesus' disciples did when He was arrested: we would run away as far as we could and seek to save our own skins at any cost. But even if we do show ourselves in this baser light on one dramatic occasion, there is still hope for our future growth into fully divine humanity. Poor Peter, who denied his Master three times, eventually reached a stage of spiritual development when he could sacrifice his life with courage in the way his Master had shown during His ministry on earth. The meaning Peter had attached to his life had risen from mere survival and the enjoyment of bodily pleasures, to the beatific vision known in a life given unconditionally to God. Paul, who relied entirely on a punctilious obedience to the Law which condemned rather than saved its devotees, had to learn about the supremacy of faith based on yielding love. "But all such assets (as the Law could provide) I have written off because of Christ. I would say more: I count everything sheer loss, because all is far outweighed by the gain of knowing Christ Jesus my Lord, for whose sake I did in fact lose everything. I count it so much garbage, for the sake of gaining Christ and finding myself incorporate in Him, with no righteousness of my own, no legal rectitude, but the righteousness which comes from faith in Christ, given by God in response to faith. All I care for is to know Christ, to experience the power of His resurrection and to share His sufferings, in growing conformity with His death, if only I may finally arrive at the resurrection from the dead" (Philippians 3:7–11).

It is in fact through this God-given faith that love springs into the heart and the works done by the person may really be good. The crucial point is that works done under the direction of the human will are perverted no matter how laudable their intention. Works that are really good spring from the heart of a person who functions, not from the ego consciousness, but from the spark of God set deeply in his soul. Such works, far from being contrived and deliberated upon, issue spontaneously from the heart. They amaze the agent no less than those to whom the work is dedicated. St Paul says: "I have been crucified with Christ: the life I now live is not my life, but the life which Christ lives in me" (Galatians 2:19). This crucifixion with Christ is enacted sacramentally at the time of baptism, but there has to come a time in the life of every person, whether or not he is a believer in God, when he is literally crucified on the cross of suffering. Only then does he come to know God, rather than merely believe in Him. And the proof of this knowledge is that the Word of God lives in him and performs the works of salvation. Every sacramental act in every religious tradition is an earnest, a presage and a preparation, for that supreme act of self-renunciation that is the essential gateway to the changed life of the person in God.

"They also serve who only stand and wait." So wrote John Milton in the last line of his moving sonnet dedicated to his blindness. The greatest of women was Mary, the mother of Jesus. She was indeed the God-bearer, for in her womb the Spirit and the flesh united completely in one body. She was chosen not because of any outward attribute or gift, but because of the purity of her heart and the openness of her spirit. In the words of the Magnificat: "the hungry he has satisfied with good things, the rich sent empty away." She was the most favoured one: the Lord was with her. When she was apprised of the role in salvation history that she was chosen to fulfil, she said: "Here am I, I am the Lord's servant; as you have spoken, so be it." Her Son was also to say: "So be it," in the moment of His greatest agony in Gethsemane not so many years later. When her time was fulfilled and the child Jesus was born, Mary's great role faded into the background. When Jesus was twelve years old He left His parents after the Passover festival in Jerusalem and tarried behind, discoursing with the teachers of the Law. When His mother remonstrated with

Him, He said to her rather perfunctorily: "Did you not know that I was bound to be in my Father's house?" She likewise was put in her place during the miracle at the marriage at Cana, in Galilee: "Your concern, mother, is not mine. My hour has not yet come" (John 2:4). In the early part of Jesus' ministry it is recorded that His mother and brothers arrived and asked Him to come out to them. He asks rhetorically: "Who is my mother, who are my brothers?" And looking round at those who are sitting in the circle about Him, He says: "Here are my mother and my brothers. Whoever does the will of God is my brother, my sister, my mother" (Mark 3:31–35). So the woman who had the supreme privilege and pain of bearing the Christ now is shown her unobtrusive place among the body of believers. But she too, in the account of the Passion according to St John, has her final moment of remembrance. When her son was being crucified, there she stood with her sister, Mary the wife of Clopas, and with Mary of Magdala. And there Jesus commends her keeping to the beloved disciple, and that disciple's welfare to her. These three women were probably the ultimate human support of Jesus in their steadfast loyalty despite the horror and the incomprehensible tragedy of the occasion. In its meaninglessness, according to the expectations of Jesus' followers, they too must have floundered in dismay. But they stayed on till the end. To Mary of Magdala was given the supreme privilege of being the first witness of the resurrected Lord. To Jesus' mother belonged the work of welding the early little community of believers together, long before they were called Christians. We meet her for the last time in the Acts of the Apostles (1:14), when the disciples came together in the upper room where they were lodging. There they prayed constantly together with a group of women, including Mary the mother of Jesus, and His brothers.

And so it is that the mother of Jesus became the mother of the earliest community that met around the resurrected Lord. When He ascended to His Father and the Holy Spirit descended upon the body of believers, she took her place as queen of the communion of saints. She is known to millions of Christians as their greatest intercessor. But more important even than this is her role in human life. Mary represents the soul, the aspect of the personality that is eternally close to God. Mary's great work is to be herself as she was, both in the moment of her greatest glory when she bore the God-man and in the time of her greatest agony when she saw her Son, of whom so much had been predicted at the time of His birth, now suffering a shameful death between two criminals. Her stillness was a part of Jesus' strength before His great descent into hell to redeem that which was lost. The spirit of contemplation is the one thing necessary for healing. When one knows this spirit one can be still before one's trial, and emerge full of the power of God's Spirit. True contemplation is a fruit of suffering and the purification which follows that travail's searing scrutiny of all our inner deviations and idolatries.

When a person is old and decrepit, there is nevertheless some meaning left in his life. He can be still and listen to those in need. The art of silent communion with another person is also the essence of the healing process. Most of us are so active about our own business that we have no time to listen even to the inner voice of God that tries to make itself heard in the depths of our being. We are about our own business, but God's business of creation and redemption simply does not enter the range of our consideration. But when we are old, superannuated and infirm, we have the remainder of the time before we die in our own hands. As long as we have a mind that can respond and senses that are able to participate meaningfully in communication with other people, let us give of ourselves as counsellors to the perplexed and distraught. To counsel means to listen and to be available to the promptings of the Holy Spirit who "fills the hungry with good things". When we are at last at home in ourselves, we can open the door of our souls to the One who knocks and has waited so long for admission. He was always there, but we were not available.

Suffering concentrates our attention on the one thing necessary for healing: the Spirit of God who alone can deliver us from the body of corruption to the place of freedom. The transition may be painful, but the destination is beyond all description in its splendour and completeness.

Meditation

Help me, O Lord, to cease from comparing my lot with that of other people, but rather to see each circumstance, however adverse, as my opportunity for growing into authentic spiritual knowledge. May I thereby be a constant source of inspiration to those around me. One true witness of sanctity is worth all the world's scriptures inasmuch as that person embodies the truth of all written testimonies.

10

Vicarious Suffering

From what I have said so far, suffering must be seen as an essential ingredient of life and a necessary way for the growth of the individual into something of a full person. Keats believed that our world was a vale of soul-making; fundamentally this is true but the concept of soul-*building* is even more accurate inasmuch as the essence of the personality, which we call the soul, is probably already there when a child is born. Indeed, the Lord said to Jeremiah: "Before I formed you in the womb, I knew you for my own; before you were born I consecrated you" (Jeremiah 1:4). This does suggest that an essence of personal identity exists before the conception of the physical body, a view apparently more acceptable to ancient Greek thought and the Hindu and Buddhist traditions than to the great Semitic monotheistic religions, except in their more esoteric versions. The latter variants are more adventurous in their metaphysical speculations but run the risk of heretical deviation. The Holy Spirit does not, however, allow us to remain for long entrenched in a complacent attitude, for he leads us on towards a full appreciation of the truth however much we may resent his intrusion in our lives.

The progressive nature of revelation is stated categorically in John 16:12–13, when Jesus is reported as saying: "There is still much that I could say to you, but the burden would be too great for you now. However, when he comes who is the Spirit of truth, he will guide you into all the truth; for he will not speak on his own authority, but will tell only what he hears, and he will make known to you the things that are coming." Whatever knowledge leads mankind into a greater commitment to God and raises the material world a little closer to its spiritual reality is mediated by the Holy Spirit. Whatever boosts the ego of the individual, making him feel special and different from his fellows so that he becomes remote from the world around him, is mediated by indeterminate psychic powers. In other words, the power of the Spirit inspires a person in the direction of his true calling as a son of God who serves and suffers on behalf of his fellow creatures in the likeness of the incarnate Christ. By contrast, the forces that emanate from the purely psychic level exalt a person above his stature in life and separate him from his fellows in a void of illusion that he mistakes for spiritual reality. His end is solitary, whereas the end of the spiritually based person is in mystical union with a transfigured world in the glory of God.

St Paul says of the Spirit: "Where the Spirit of the Lord is, there is liberty. And because for us there is no veil over the face we all reflect as in a mirror the splendour of the Lord; thus we are transfigured into his likeness, from splendour to splendour; such is the influence of the Lord who is Spirit" (II Corinthians 3:17–18). This is especially true of the person who has traversed the path of suffering and come out on the other side in the light of a renewed life — "for this son of mine was dead, and has come back to life; he was lost and is found" (Luke 15:24). How does the life of a person who has passed over the valley of the shadow of death differ from the life he once led as an unawakened individual? The awakened person is inspired by God's spirit to love with an ardour that is out of all comparison to the passion of an unawakened sensual man. The love that most people know is a selfish emotional attachment; it is a demanding attitude that keeps the beloved bound to the desires of the one who loves. It has strongly possessive undertones, and the centre of the love is the selfish, clinging need of the lover. We all yearn for the security of a deep relationship with someone whom we like and believe we can trust, but if we are not constantly vigilant, we and the other person can become imprisoned in chains of mutual dependence. The result of the distressingly common egoistical attachment that masquerades as love is that neither individual is allowed to grow into what God has determined for him, the measure of a full person.

Of course, even those early strivings for a deeper relationship between two unaware people are not to be summarily dismissed. Even the first groping after the support of another person broadens the ego-centred limitations of an isolated existence sufficiently to embrace the concerns of another human being. This is how the individual's awareness grows in even superficial acquaintanceships, until he can form closer friendships which may find their summation in a life-long marriage relationship. But even in such a situation it is not very unusual for the two partners hardly to know one another in any depth even after a considerable number of years together. The reason for this lack of intimate communion is that neither partner has any deep knowledge of the self. Indeed, much social intercourse is conducted with the implicit purpose of shielding everyone involved from too deep an involvement with the issues that really matter. Words skilfully used can deflect us from a real experience of the other person while focussing our attention away from our own basic insecurity. Thus we skate skilfully on a smooth surface of inconsequential living until the ice cracks and we are submerged in the freezing waters of real life. This is the moment of truth when all our illusions — especially the false relationships we have shared with our fellow creatures — are shattered and we are left floundering in a sea of suffering, groping desperately for some solid support on which to cling. There is, of course, only one such source of support, the Lord of life. When we know Him, we begin the essential change for which we were created — to put off the purely human, evanescent nature and to be transformed progressively into the divine nature. The first indication of this change is a renewed love for life, but of a quality far different from anything we had previously known.

The ability to love freely and in a non-attached, transpersonal way is especially the fruit of the successful journey

through psychic darkness of the intensity that Jesus experienced alone in the Garden of Gethsemane when those
three disciples whom He had chosen for their special closeness
to Him — Peter, James and John — slept on in uncomprehending stupor. The person who, like Jesus, emerges battered
but entire from this most harrowing of all encounters with the
collective power of evil, can never sleep again when even one
of the least of his brethren is in distress. "I tell you this:
anything you did for one of my brothers here, however
humble, you did for me" (Matthew 25:40). Perhaps this reflection contrasts the love of one who has been renewed in
God after losing everything that he once held important from
the sporadic feelings of goodwill and charity that enter the
hearts of many unawakened people during the course of their
lives. To do the occasional kindly action is not only appropriate but it also lightens the burden of an ego-centred
existence. To be eternally about our Father's business and in
His house, as Jesus saw His work even at the age of twelve,
means that the ego has been permanently and absolutely
demoted from its natural seat of dominance and is now the
servant of the Lord who is Spirit. It is in this spirit that Jesus'
words to His self-seeking disciples have an eternal meaning:
"You know that in the world the recognised rulers lord it over
their subjects, and their great men make them feel the weight
of authority. This is not the way with you; among you, whoever
wants to be great must be your servant, and whoever wants to
be first must be the willing slave of all. For even the Son of
Man did not come to be served, but to serve, and to give up
His life as a ransom for many" (Mark 10:42–45).

The one who has emerged a changed person from the valley
of suffering has passed beyond the thraldom of striving for
greatness and power. Having lost everything the world holds
dear, including the identity one previously had, for Christ's
sake and for the Gospel, one has indeed found eternal life,
which is the centre within oneself that is inviolable against all
the inroads of material ruin or psychic eruption. In this respect

anyone who has prevailed against the onslaught of unremitting
suffering and dark despair is a messenger of God's Word and
Gospel irrespective of his religious background. He has done
the will of the heavenly Father and the kingdom of Heaven is
his. This is not true of the arrogant type of believer who calls
"Lord, Lord" vociferously but avoids any damaging involvement in the world's tragedies or in the suffering of his fellow
creatures. It is to the servants of humanity, who have been
changed by the refining fire of suffering, that the Son of Man
will say: "You have my Father's blessing; come, enter and
possess the kingdom that has been ready for you since the
world was made" (Matthew 25:34). An unawakened person
cannot fulfil the social and communal demands set out in the
Parable of the Sheep and the Goats. Only those who have
dispensed with a purely personal life and have entered the
transpersonal way in God can be eternally about their Father's
business — which means caring for the hungry and thirsty,
the stranger and the prisoner, and all who are sick. And this
caring is no mere welfare work such as is nowadays increasingly
being relegated to various professional agencies. The caring
of the one who is centred in God is a constant awareness of the
deepest sufferings of other people, so that they are remem-
bered in prayer when one is away from them no less than
enveloped in love when one is in their bodily presence. In this
respect caring for someone is not the same as loving him. Care
brings resources to a person in distress; love gives oneself to
him. It is impossible to love a person without caring deeply for
him; in the Parable of the Good Samaritan, the central figure
of the story combined love and care in the relief he afforded to
the unfortunate man who had fallen among thieves on the
road from Jerusalem to Jericho. On the other hand, care can
be very impersonal especially when it is meted out by agencies
of social welfare and there is no impulse of love behind it.
Care divested of love's ardour soon assumes the burden of a
duty or even the arrogance of an act of condescension. How
sad it is that that most excellent word "charity", purer than

many versions of love currently in use, is popularly identified
with almsgiving. No wonder it is often described as cold!

Jesus made some hard demands on His disciples. After He
had sent the rich young man away with the recommendation
to sell all he had and give it to the poor and then to come and
follow Him, a counsel of perfection that affected the youth
with profound depression as he withdrew from the Master,
Jesus told those around Him how impossible it was for anyone
clinging to riches to enter God's kingdom. The amazement
with which the disciples greeted this teaching is both amusing
and salutary; it was commonly believed that wealth was a
reward for good living and misfortune a punishment from
God for wrongful actions. This view is still the popular one
today, as is seen in the superfical teaching given by many who
are involved in the ministry of healing. Jesus had compassion
on the disciples when they protested against the harshness of
His demands and said: "Then who can be saved?" The answer
was clear and decisive: "For men it is impossible, but not for
God; everything is possible for God" (Mark 10:17–27). *This is
the heart of the matter. Only the man who has emerged from the
dark pit of suffering is able to live no more in himself but in
God.* To repeat St Paul's insight: "I have been crucified with
Christ: the life I now live is not my life, but the life which
Christ lives in me" (Galatians 2:20). This is, of course, part of
a typical conversion experience, and as such has been known
by many believers in their path to a full commitment to Christ.
But it remains merely a dramatic presage of future glory until
the life of a believer has, in the course of withering suffering,
been so transformed that his personality bears the marks of
the crucified Lord and shines with the light of His resurrected
body. What St Paul glimpsed in the many moments of illumination that punctuated the writing of his inspired letters had
to be actualised in life by his becoming a changed person, one
who could see even his failure to be healed of his "thorn in the
flesh" as a part of the divine plan, whose strength is made
perfect in weakness. This strength in weakness was manifested

once and for all time in the crucifixion of Jesus. As He descended into hell, so He initiated the release from that sordid psychic atmosphere of all those who had lain incarcerated in its hopeless, meaningless chaos of darkness since the creation of the world.

When one ponders on these sombre yet liberating thoughts, so the paradox of the suffering servant described in Isaiah 53 approaches an existential solution: by this I mean a solution based on the experience of common life, not on metaphysical speculations. Indeed, I suspect that the well-meaning agnostic philosophers of our world inhabit their special domain on the periphery of heaven but outside its bounds, where they continue to argue interminably about the meaning of life and the existence of God. Only those who have found a meaning to their lives in surmounting the suffering of the created universe will know indisputably that God does indeed exist. And they will know Him eternally in the atmosphere of Heaven, not only as an intimate personal presence beyond definition but also as the boundless, timeless expanse of unitive love in which all creation lives and moves and has its being.

In Isaiah 53 we read: "He grew up before the Lord like a young plant whose roots are in parched ground; he had no beauty, no majesty to draw our eyes, no grace to make us delight in him; his form, disfigured, lost all the likeness of a man, his beauty changed beyond all human semblance. He was despised, he shrank from the sight of men, tormented and humbled by suffering; we despised him, we held him of no account, a thing from which men turn away their eyes. Yet on himself he bore our sufferings, our torments he endured, while we counted him smitten by God, struck down by disease and misery; but he was pierced for our transgressions, tortured for our iniquities; the chastisement he bore is health for us and by his scourging we are healed" (verses 2–5). The important point to realise about this famous passage, one of the greatest insights into the nature of God that has ever entered the imagination of a human mind, is that the servant on whom all suffering is poured is the most privileged of men. He, in identifying himself with the sores and dregs of life, has been identified with God also, who entered fully into the world at the moment His Word uttered the creative command, and who entered personally into the darkest tragedy of life at the time of the Incarnation of Christ. It was for this very end that man was created: to raise up all that is mortal in our world to immortality, all that is corrupt to incorruption. But to perform this act of transfiguration the master has to become the servant; indeed lower than the most menial slave, he has to identify himself with mortality and corruption sufficiently to love it and die for it. Only then does the process of healing begin. And the servant is resurrected into life eternal as he raises up the dead and glorifies the sordid dregs of degraded humanity.

This is the real ministry of healing. It is strongly related to the Sacrament of Baptism. As St Paul reminded his Roman brethren: "Have you not forgotten that when we were baptised into union with Jesus Christ we were baptised into His death? By baptism we were buried with Him, and lay dead in order that, as Christ was raised from the dead in the splendour of the Father, so also we might set our feet upon the new path of life" (Romans 6:3-4). Jesus reminds His followers of the supreme baptism when they look for honours in the world to come: "Can you drink the cup that I drink, or be baptised with the baptism I am baptised with?" (Mark 10:38). The disciples affirm that they can, and indeed they prove it in their sub-sequent ministry, but they little knew what they were assuming when they made their first declaration of fidelity. They first had to experience disillusionment, despair, a full knowledge of their own wretchedness in their rejection of their Master when He needed them most, and then the forgiveness that comes as grace from God. Only then could they follow in the way and be filled with the Holy Spirit to do the great work of continuing Jesus' mission to the world. In this way what is presented first to the newly-fledged believer as a sacrament of death and resurrection is finally fulfilled in his own life as an experience of personal death and spiritual resurrection. Only the resurrected one can be a full instrument of the healing power of God's Spirit.

When one suffers on behalf of someone else, one takes his burden on oneself and lifts it up to God. The Holy Spirit flows into the soul of the one who offers himself as a sacrifice for the world, and transforms both the burden and the one who has chosen the way of self-giving. To be the instrument of trans-figuring the pain of the world into joy means that every base, mean, selfish impulse in one's own life must first be similarly transfigured. It is the cold wind and acrid stench of psychic dark-ness that cleanses one prior to the act of transfiguration, which is effected by the Holy Spirit penetrating the very marrow of one's being. As one is changed from the previously convention-ally respectable figure in the world's eyes to something that is unmentionably foul, so a new type of beauty permeates one's being, a beauty seen outwardly in the stigmata of Christ and inwardly as a transfiguring radiance which embraces the whole creation, having nothing outside its orbit, nothing isolated or rejected. Indeed, we are all healed as a result of his scourging.

An intimation of this universal healing has been given by some people who have passed through hell and emerged un-scathed in inner integrity. I am always reminded of a particular prayer that was found on a piece of wrapping paper near the body of a dead child in Ravensbruck Nazi Concentration Camp, where it is estimated that 92,000 women and children died;

O Lord
Remember not only the men and women of goodwill,
but also those of illwill.
But do not only remember the suffering they have
                                    inflicted on us,
remember the fruits we bought, thanks to this suffering,
our comradeship, our loyalty, our humility,
the courage, the generosity,

the greatness of heart which has grown out of all this,
and when they come to judgement,
let all the fruits that we have borne be their forgiveness.

In this almost unbearably moving testament of forgiveness,
we can glimpse the inner meaning of the doctrine of the
Atonement. In some respects this document, written almost
certainly by one who was not a Christian, comes closer to the
heart of the mystery of this doctrine than either the "satisfaction" theory of St Anselm or the "substitution" theory of
John Calvin, because its centre is pure love without the demand
for justice (on the human level) to be satisfied. Of course, the
sacrifice of himself this transfigured person in the prison camp
freely gave is not of the same order as that prophesied in
Isaiah 53 with regard to the suffering servant or manifested by
Christ in His death and passion. For those latter two were
completely sinless, being infused with the presence of God,
whereas even the noblest victim of the prison camps of our
own time would have confessed to many shortcomings prior
to the terrible ordeal that so transformed him. But the essential
quality he would share with Jesus is that of offering himself
without reservation in order to save the wicked from the fruits
of their own destructive actions. Once they have been so
saved, I believe the wicked would, like the Prodigal Son,
come to themselves and start a new life of service to God and
love to their fellows, whether in this world or in the greater life
beyond death. It is this trust in the ultimately redeeming
power of love that convinces me that everything in the creative
process will come to its own fulfilment in God, transfigured
and resurrected.

Only when one has been through the hell that Jesus endured
and emerged transfigured, can one appreciate and bear with
Christ the hell of another person. Even if one has not undergone exactly the same experience as He has, one is still fully
conscious of the intense pain that underlies it, and one can
at least share it with him. Carl Jung said on one occasion that

only the wounded surgeon heals. This is especially true of those who, in their own form, bear the stigmata of the Lord. Jesus experienced every psychic hell known to man in the Gethsemane experience. Later on the cross at Golgotha He was to partake of extreme physical agony also. It is in this way that His presence is with everyone who suffers; the individual situation varies but the underlying pain, dread, despair and spiritual obfuscation are shared in common.

Blaise Pascal wrote: "Jesus will be in agony until the end of the world: all that time we must not sleep" (*Pensée* 736). His vigil and ours — unlike His three sleeping disciples — will continue until every sentient creature is relieved of pain and distress so that it too can enter the heavenly bliss of God's presence with us. So close is all life in solidarity that no individual can pass beyond the point of no return to suffering while even a single tiny creature is in distress. In one esoteric Buddhist text, the Bodhisattva (the Enlightened One who has passed beyond the wheel of rebirth and can now enter the eternal bliss of Nirvana) hears these words: "Can there be bliss when all that lives must suffer? Shalt thou be saved and hear the whole world cry?" (This comes from the *Book of the Golden Precepts* in an annotated version entitled *The Voice of the Silence*). He renounces Nirvana until all beings can enter into its bliss with him, when indeed the world of becoming (Samsara) and the world of reality (Nirvana) are one. What the highest Buddhist intuition recognised as the ultimate truth of renunciation was realised by the crucified Christ. At this point these two great spiritual traditions merge, fuse and become one in the Godhead, which is beyond all names and concepts.

It is not infrequently asserted by students of the occult that so great a Master as Jesus need not have suffered pain or despair on the cross. Surely He was also a master of psychical, occult techniques by which He could have lifted His consciousness from the agony of his body to the bliss of His spiritual nature. Whether or not He knew of such techniques is neither here nor there; one thing is, however, certain. It was contingent upon Him to identify Himself completely with His human brethren. Only by bearing their pain could He enter fully into the lives of even the most menial, degraded people. And following this complete identification with mankind at its most sordid and tragic, Jesus is eternally available to bear the suffering of all who work in obscure faith and are open to the inflow of divine grace even when, like Jesus on the cross, they call out, "My God, My God, why hast thou forsaken me ?"

This statement of the necessity for bearing the pain of all creation is not to be seen as a self-indulgent revelling in suffering and humiliation. It is well known that some psychologically disturbed people get considerable satisfaction from their misery. This state of masochism has unconscious sexual roots, and is clearly an attitude of mind that is to be deprecated. Furthermore, it is possible to escape life's present demands by relapsing into ill-health or emotional instability. The hysterical type of person uses this way of escape, albeit unconsciously, whenever confronted with a severe test of present decision or endurance. As was recorded in John 5:1–9, when a certain man who had been crippled for thirty-eight years but had never been able to enter the healing waters of Bethesda in time, was confronted by Jesus, he was asked quite directly: "Do you want to recover?" Jesus obviously divined a basic ambivalence in the crippled man's attitude to being healthy once more. *He* had to make the decision, as we all must do in our crises. God does not thrust health on us any more than suffering. It is part of the life we have been given that we should participate in both these experiences, but if we are open to God, our inevitable periods of darkness will be blessed by the presence of the suffering Christ, so that we may emerge from the deep pit of pain stronger, more compassionate, and a little closer to the likeness of our Lord. It is only then that we will know the resurrected Christ, who will be the agent of an even more splendid outwardly manifested healing. Of course, the way of suffering and the experience of healing are essentially dual aspects of the path of human endeavour, just as the suffering Christ is the same person as the resurrected Lord.

The way of courageous suffering leads to a new life in God. Morbid, introspective suffering can be a very effective way of evading the challenge of life to know ourselves as we really are. It can be a way, not so very different in its final effect of averting the gaze of the individual from the true self, that is accomplished more frequently and pleasurably by superficial entertainment, shallow conversation and sensual stimulation. The person who can bear the suffering of another is not a sentimentalist who flows out in words of sympathy. Such an approach can lead to both of them wallowing in the pain and injustice of life and perhaps feeling superior to those who do not suffer. To bear another's pain means to be constantly present in thought and prayer, silent except when moved to speak by the Holy Spirit, always aware of the depth of distress and yet even more conscious of the power and light of God, who rules omnipotently in all worlds and over all situations. Such a person suffers vicariously, and in taking on the victim's burdens gives them to God in prayer. And God transfigures both the victim and the intercessor while changing the burden from an unbearable tragedy to a presage of triumph.

There are some people engaged in a healing ministry who claim such a degree of psychic rapport with those on whom they bestow their healing gift that they feel they pick up the diseased condition of their patient. They experience pain, perhaps in a similar area of the body to that of the patient. If these claims are factually true, and a healthy agnosticism is essential in their evaluation, they simply point to a close psychic sensitivity on the part of the agent of healing. In themselves they are neither indications of special spirituality nor do they necessarily help the other person. Indeed, they can be dangerous both in depleting the health of the one who ministers healing and in inflating his ego. This psychic sensitivity is not to be equated with vicarious suffering, though the one who does suffer for another will assuredly be in the closest psychic communion with him. This is an interesting example of both the connection between the psychic and spiritual dimensions of relationship and their great difference. Psychic sensitivity, if it is not inspired by God, merely brings two people into a close emotional relationship which may just as easily be destructive as healing. But the one who is the true agent of vicarious suffering has been so changed through his own deep experience of hell and resurrection that he has, as it were, left his ego behind and is a pure servant of God. To quote St Paul for a third time: "I have been crucified with Christ: the life I now live is not my life, but the life which Christ lives in me" (Galatians 2:20). This is the life of vicarious suffering. By that life others are truly brought into healing relationship with God.

The meaning of this change to divine consciousness is brought out in a famous passage from the Letter to the Hebrews (5:7–10), which refers to the suffering of Christ that was a necessary precursor of His subsequent glorification. "In the days of His earthly life He offered up prayers and petitions, with loud cries and tears, to God who was able to deliver Him from the grave. Because of His humble submission, His prayer was heard: Son though He was, He learned obedience in the school of suffering, and once perfected, became the source of eternal salvation for all who obey Him, named by God high priest in the succession of Melchizedek." Even Jesus, though of divine nature, had to have His humanity perfected in the school of suffering, which is the everyday world where the common people lead their alternatively depressing, boring, depraved and heroic lives. The end of this process of perfection was begun in Gethsemane and brought to a triumphant conclusion in the underworld of hell. The means to this end was unremitting love. In weakness the strength of God was shown to the world, and in love death was overcome in victory. The heart of this is unreserved forgiveness.

Meditation

It is in giving of oneself freely that one begins to learn who one really is: a child of God created in the image of the God-man Jesus Christ. The end of this self-knowledge is the raising of all life to the likeness of God through the mediation of Christ. God became man in order that man might become God, as St Athanasius put it so succinctly and perfectly.

11

The Suffering in Relationships: the Pain of Perfection

Amongst those experiences of life from which there is no escape is the awareness that you have fallen from the high standard that you know is a full measure of yourself. This falling from the mark, the evasion of the call to be true to one's highest intimations of reality which are codified in the moral teachings of the Bible, is the inner meaning of sin. Its outer showing is a perverse attitude to other people. It is of the essence of the paradox of human nature that we are both set a high standard of perfection and constantly betraying it in our lives. The heart of this paradox lies in the contrast between what we really are, children of God, and the journey away from that true identity we are obliged to make in the course of our life.

The history of Israel as recounted throughout the Old Testament is also an allegorical account of the soul's journey in time. The first of our human compatriots, Adam and Eve, are unconsciously living in unity with God and the created universe; they do not know God and are unaware of themselves as people. It is only when they disobey the command from above and partake of the fruit of human, divisive knowledge that their eyes are opened and they begin to see themselves as isolated creatures. At the same time, they have to confront their separation from God and their exclusion from the full life in eternity. The first Adam becomes a living soul, finite and isolated. His primal sin has emphasised the grasping, unscrupulous, predatory tendencies in man, intent only on himself with no regard for those around him. And yet he cannot ignore his true nature nor be unmindful of the destiny that he dimly divines within himself.

The great figures in the Book of Genesis — Noah, Abraham,

Isaac, Jacob and Joseph — are more than simply characters in an historical setting. They are archetypes of the obedience of man to his divine calling in the wisdom of God. They show the pattern of right human relationships with God in which man is fully human and God both transcends all human understanding and yet is deeply rooted in His creation: His voice speaks in man's deepest intuition and gives the divine command to leave the flesh-pots of immediate gratification and enter into a way that is not known by human reason. The instruction given to Moses in Exodus 25:40 concerning the building of the tabernacle is even more pertinent to the saints of humanity in their relationship to the pattern of mankind's strivings to perfection: "See that you work to the design which you were shown on the mountain." The archetypes are our design, and we see them most clearly on the mountain of illumination when we put darkness behind us and view reality without impediment.

In the enthralling story of the exodus of the Israelites from Egypt under the leadership of Moses, we see a development of human consciousness beyond absorption in archetypal figures to a full participation in life. The Law brought down symbolically by Moses from Mount Sinai is the bond that unites God and man. It is in fulfilling the law of God that man participates in God's perpetual labour in the world; it is man's supreme privilege to work with God in the maintenance and spiritualisation of the created universe, at least inasmuch as it embraces our small place in it, though no one can know the extent of the cosmos that may respond to prayer. It is, as it were, that the exodus event marks man's arrival at an adult state of self-awareness. He sees himself in the world responsible for himself and his surroundings and privileged to commune with God and do the work that God requires. But the vision slips away time after time. The tempestuous rejections and apostasies of the Israelites in the wilderness bring on them appropriate punishment, and only after a prolonged period of purification is this turbulent people seen to be worthy of inheriting the promised land. The remainder of the Old Testament is a development of the theme of election by God, a slow striving for spiritual mastery, victory, apostasy, suffering and destruction. A remnant is left to continue the work, and every peak of triumph ends on a mute note of disillusionment, disintegration and destruction. This is not merely the story of a peculiar people: it is mankind's story, of whom Israel is the supreme representative. It is repeated in one form or another in all the world's religions, even the Christian religion, despite the radically new departure heralded by the God-man Jesus Christ, who of all the great spiritual figures in the world's history, gained victory in defeat, transfigured degradation to glory, and showed a full resurrection of even corruptible physical elements.

In the mystical views of ultimate reality there are several strands, none of which is adequate on its own, but all of which contribute to a fuller understanding of the life which we, as ordinary people, have to experience. This life is a mosaic of happiness and suffering, of growth and death. In the Advaita, non-dualistic philosophy of Shankara, the One alone is real. The relationship with the One (or Brahman) and the soul is that of pure, simple identity. All that is fleeting and changing, which is the realm of finite experience and is subject to time and multiplicity, is unreal. It is illusory (or maya). It is ignorance (avidya) that is the root of the illusory appearance of finite things, although even this false appearance of the reality of the finite springs from the power of Brahman. In this respect Brahman is not the same as the personal God worshipped in the Semitic monotheistic religions. Brahman is more akin to the ineffable Godhead that can be described only in terms of what it is not, since it transcends all rational categories. And yet it is open to all in the supreme mystical illumination that is man's privilege to experience if only he were humble and receptive. It is known to the mystic as being, awareness and bliss. This ultimate reality is what each creature is in essence, since the spark of the soul, the Atman, is one with

Brahman. The Buddhist doctrine of the void is another expression of this great insight into reality.

However this extreme monism does not fit in with the whole gamut of experience. Other great mystics, while acknowledging supreme reality only to the One whom men call God, also accept that the creation has its own integrity. There is a hierarchy of created forms that are differentiated individually without being divided one from the other. St Paul's analogy of the body of Christ, in which each member is an essential organ yet unable to exist except in the unity of the whole body, is a valuable illustration of this truth. Our particular world may be a dark universe in the hierarchy of heavenly realms; it may indeed be a shadow-world, but it has its own significance in the scheme of things. It is not simply an illusion. This is the Platonic insight which was fully articulated in the mystical theology of Plotinus. Indeed, the experience of the soul's separateness and isolation is a surface phenomenon, for in the depths of being the separation dissolves in the living reality of God.

The Indian mystic Ramanuja, the exponent of modified non-dualism and a critic of the great Shankara, believed that the obviously manifold nature of the universe springs from a tendency inherent in the very nature of divine reality. Both he and Plotinus saw man as a young prince brought up among strangers, unaware of his own origin or his true nature. Indeed, he cannot be or know himself until he acknowledges his inner oneness with God. Ignorance lies at the root of this human alienation, and the basis of the misunderstanding is the false identification of the person with his body, which should be his servant but which has, in the course of incarnate life, become his master.

This essential insight into the dilemma of human consciousness can easily enter extreme dimensions. The gnostics believed (as we have noted already) that matter was intrinsically evil, indeed that the material world was itself the outcome of a fall. Matter can asssume, in this outlook, a force of blind desire, a manifestation of the power of darkness which is in perpetual conflict with the divine power of light. Some gnostic mystics attribute evil to the operation of forces beyond worldly limitation, even indeed as a result of discord arising among the divine qualities. The great Jewish theosophical treatise, the *Zohar* which is the heart of Kabbalah, sees discord arising through the separation of divine judgement (Din or Gevurah) and divine mercy and love (Hesed).

All this may seem dry and barren, purely intellectual speculation, but throughout human history the greatest minds have wrestled with the problem of evil and the destiny of the universe. Both are different aspects of the same enigma. As far as my own insight has shown it to me, I have no doubt that God is in control. All the schemes alluded to have their validity in the total reality of life in God. None is completely adequate on its own, but each complements the unsatisfied part of its fellow. To return to the analogy of the human soul among strangers, which seems to be a profound insight into the human condition, it seems that this very experience of alienation is necessary for the growth of the person into full union with God. While the monistic view of the identity of the soul and the One is eternally true, this truth has to be experienced, not philosophically or even in a fleeting mystical experience, but in the course of incarnate life. It is through the experience of suffering that is at the heart of all separative existence, as the Buddha so rightly diagnosed the human condition, that man transcends the purely personal mode of being and enters his true estate. He is indeed a prince by birth, but before he can enjoy the privilege and responsibility of his inheritance, he has to prove himself worthy. And the seal of worthiness consists in knowing the world, knowing its creatures, identifying himself with all of them, and sacrificing himself for them. Only then are the scales lifted from his eyes, and he can enter into the royal realm which is the kingdom of God.

There was One alone who showed this pattern in His short life, and He entered the state of resurrection after He had given everything He had in order to redeem all that was lost and forgotten by men. Through faith all who believe in Him are shown the way to eternal life in God and are strengthened by His Spirit. But they have to recapitulate the life of their Lord. Mere intellectual acceptance of credal formulae is not the essence of the faith that saves. That faith offers itself as a living sacrifice to God and to be used as God wills it. Thus the faith that Abraham had was not fully shown until he entered on the final act of actually preparing to slay his son Isaac; only then did God intervene supernaturally, and a new understanding of reality was granted to the great patriarch. The metaphysical identity of the spirit of man with the One is realised in bodily life only when man has, in the likeness of Christ, raised up into glory all that is corrupt and fallen in the world.

Suffering *is* the way of growth into Christhood, and our sufferings complement the redemptive work of Christ on the cross. As St Paul says: "It is now my happiness to suffer for you. This is my way of helping to complete, in my poor human flesh, the full tale of Christ's afflictions still to be endured, for the sake of his body which is the church" (Colossians 1:24). This does not mean that St Paul's suffering adds to the value of Christ's redemptive work, for this work could not be augmented. It means that the pain we must all undergo for the kingdom of God to be established on earth is our contribution to the resurrection of the world, since "the universe itself is to be freed from the shackles of mortality and enter upon the liberty and splendour of the children of God" (Romans 8:21). This is perhaps St Paul's supreme insight concerning the full meaning of the Incarnation and its final end. It is our privilege to be God's heirs and Christ's co-heirs as we share His sufferings now in order to share His splendour hereafter (Romans 8:17).

Simone Weil expressed the vocation of suffering in Christ perfectly when she wrote: "The extreme greatness of Christianity lies in the fact that it does not seek a supernatural remedy for suffering but a supernatural use for it" (in the chapter on affliction in *Gravity and Grace*). There is no growth without pain; there is no freedom without renunciation; there is no life without perpetual death. It is the *status quo* that hems us in with the comfortable illusion of ownership that we identify with reality. This is the illusory path that the mystics are at such pains to expose and extinguish. As Jesus said: "Whoever cares for his own safety is lost; but if a man will let himself be lost for my sake, and for the Gospel, that man is safe" (Mark 8:35). Material safety is the one certain illusion, for all manifest things pass away as in a night. But the material world is our place of experience and experimentation. We grow into full human beings in its environment, as we, in our turn, have to give something of our essence to lift up the rocks and soil, the vegetation and the animal creation, and indeed the very air we breathe, from inertia to life and from the cycle of decay and death to eternal life. Only then does the world around us live with us, and both we and it pass from illusion to reality, from death to immortality. As we grow into spiritual understanding, so we begin to grasp the essential truth that nothing is evil in itself, but anything, even the highest religious observance, can assume an evil propensity if it makes us feel that we have attained the end of our journey, that we have finally arrived. "For here we have no permanent home, but we are seekers after the city which is to come" (Hebrews 13:14). It is in coming to a measure of full humanity in the form and person of Christ that we raise up inert matter to spiritual essence and deliver that which was used for evil intent to the fully pure.

The life we lead here is one of constant imperfection. As St Paul wrote: "The good which I want to do, I fail to do; but what I do is the wrong which is against my will; and if what I do is against my will, clearly it is no longer I who am the agent, but sin that has its lodging in me. I discover this principle, then; that when I want to do the right, only the wrong is within my reach. In my inmost self I delight in the law of God, but I perceive that there is in my bodily members, the law of sin. Miserable creature that I am, who is there to rescue me out of this body doomed to death? God alone, through Jesus Christ our Lord" (Romans 7:19–25). The way of God's salvation in Christ is much more gradual and progressive than many believers, young in the Christian faith, recognise. Dramatic conversion and charismatic experiences may punctuate the inner healing that a knowledge of God brings with it, but there are also the prolonged, significant periods of apparent stagnation and relapse that are the more real way of spiritual growth. Our inner feelings are poor guides to the state of our spiritual health. The Pharisee in the famous parable thanked God that he was so much better than his fellows, whereas the tax-gatherer knew only how derelict he was, yet it was he, not the self-righteous man, who went home acquitted of his sins.

The pain of sin, which, as St Paul points out with the authority of a modern psychologist, is an integral part of natural man, manifests itself by an awareness of guilt. This is the inability to look one's fellow in the face because of one's sense of inner corruption. Not all guilt is the fruit of sin; some is due to our failure to live up to the demands exacted on us by society. This includes our parents and teachers who assume a god-like role in our lives by virtue of the conditioning they laid upon us during the formative years of childhood. This Freudian "super-ego" has to be analysed, seen in its rightful perspective, and then transcended. A guilt that derives from the unfulfilled demands of the super-ego is morbid, and it may require intelligent professional help to disentangle and exorcise.

Another dimension of society that may inflict a burden of guilt on the unfortunate person is the peer group to which he belongs. Group loyalty, which can be extended into the categories of class structure, religious affiliation and political alignment, often afflicts the sensitive person with a sense of utter worthlessness if he dares to strike out on an independent course. To be ostracised by one's former friends and colleagues is a terrifying experience. Jesus underwent this during the last period of His life when He appeared discredited in the hands of the authorities whom most of the population detested.

There is, however, a third type of guilt that is undoubtedly the fruit of sin. It occurs when we have deliberately or unwittingly betrayed a fellow human being. A stench emanates psychically from us, and we are even more aware of the radical nature of our withdrawal from the society of men than are those whom we have wronged. This is indeed an aspect of the sin against the Holy Spirit, for when we betray or demean any person, we are demeaning Christ Himself ("I tell you this: everything you did for one of my brothers here, however humble, you did for me" — Matthew 25:40); this text applies as much to someone we hurt as someone we help, since all of us are parts of one body (Ephesians 4:25). Indeed, we exclude ourselves from the one body, the living power of which is the Holy Spirit. Until we align ourselves once more with the one whom we have wronged, we cannot be in alignment with the body of mankind, and the Holy Spirit does not inspire us with life. The result is disease and death.

The reverse side of the experience of guilt for wrongful actions against other people is the equally destructive awareness of resentment over wrongs that we ourselves have suffered. If the first experience requires forgiveness for its healing, the second attitude can be repaired only by our own ability to forgive others. Forgiveness, furthermore, is of God, not of man. The religious folk of Jesus' time were quite right to be affronted by the emphatic way in which He forgave the sins of those who were afflicted in body and mind. But they were unaware of the divine nature of the One who forgave. Before we can forgive we have to experience forgiveness ourselves, and that can occur only in an encounter with God. Then God speaks through us, effecting our own inner healing and proclaiming the healing of those who have wronged us. Forgiveness brings the wrong-doer and the victim together in one body. In this body both are transformed, and a new life is available to them. The gesture of forgiveness that may be proffered on purely human terms seldom effects any change in attitude either in the victim or the guilty party. It is essentially an act of condescension, in which the one who expresses his forgiveness is really proclaiming his moral and spiritual superiority over the person who has done him an injury. To know all may be to forgive all, according to the well-known saying, but this all-embracing knowledge must include not only the circumstances of the trouble but also the persons involved. Only God can have this knowledge. As we do not even begin to know ourselves except in the pit of suffering, we are hardly in a position to know anyone else or the circumstances of either his or our own wrong-doing.

In the agony of guilt and the fury of resentment, through the muttered prayers for relief, there comes a time when the suffering is so severe that all personal demands are shattered. It is in the crucible of God's devouring fire that the old personality is completely remoulded so as to be divested of all its ego-dominated dross. Then, at last, the pearl of great price, the soul with its enshrined spark of spirit, lies revealed, and from it a new personality is born, in which the ego is a true reflection of the glory within instead of being an independent focus of domination. The devouring fire of God is also His forgiveness. It is as if we, like Jacob, have had a hard contest with the brightness of God's truth that penetrates and pulver-ises all personal illusions. When we stand naked before God's fire, His love can enter our hearts, and we can articulate His forgiveness. We know that we are forgiven because we are now as open to the world as we were in the innocence of our childhood. We have been told that only those who accept the kingdom of God like a child can ever enter it (Mark 10:15). Suffering has the cleansing effect of shattering our selfish demands for justice and rewards for services rendered. It makes us value life as the supreme gift of God. What does a man gain by winning the whole world at the cost of his true self? What can he give to buy that self back? These two piercing questions of Jesus (Mark 8:36–37) focus our attention on the reality of life itself and lead us away from dissipating our energy on the superficial events that colour and distort true living. Only the one who has suffered can separate the living reality from the illusions that encompass it. He alone is forgiven of his many sins, and the proof of that forgiveness lies in his changed attitude to those who have wronged him. He now realises, perhaps to his surprise, that he bears no one a grudge any more, that any demand for justice and retribution is completely irrelevant to the new life upon which he has entered.

This absolution from past sins does not free us from the consequences of hurtful actions that we may have committed. On the contrary, it is only with a healed conscience that we can begin to lead a risen life, one that is devoted to all the injured, sick members of society. The motivating power in putting right some of the damage we have previously done is neither a sense of duty nor the demands of society; it is a burning love that embraces all creation. It will never rest until it has lifted to resurrection all that is unclean, perverse, sordid and evil. Only when the unclean, evil thing is embraced in the love that Jesus had for those who persecuted and reviled Him can it too be reclaimed and brought back to its source, which is God. When we see forgiveness in this light, the great ethical demands of the Sermon on the Mount cease to be merely ideal attitudes of a perfect society, but become the only way in which life can be preserved. "Do not set yourself against the man who wrongs you. If someone slaps you on the right cheek, turn and offer him your left . . . Love your enemies and pray for your persecutors . . . There must be no limit to your goodness, as your heavenly Father's goodness knows no bounds" (Matthew 5:38–48).

It must be said that this counsel of perfection does not come to fruition until we have been divested of every illusion of separative existence and personal eminence by the winnowing fire of suffering. This may take the form of years of incarceration in an inhuman prison camp, or the prolonged spiritual isolation that follows the death of a loved one, or the gradually failing power of the body that accompanies progressive, incurable disease. With God's grace the suffering may end before the person dies, in which event he can show his love to the world. But more frequently his love pours out of a dying body that is a witness both to man's inhumanity to man and man's unconquerable spirit in the face of unmitigated hell. When one reads such a book as the already-mentioned *Man's Search for Meaning* by Viktor Frankl, one is struck by its transcendence of personal bitterness and by the absence of imprecations of hatred against the Nazi torturers. And yet there is no sentimentality about it which might tend to blur essential moral issues. Good and evil are clearly defined, and yet forgiveness transcends both of them and brings them into a new creative synthesis. The Buddha taught us a long time ago that hatred never ceases by hatred. Hatred ceases only by love; this is the eternal law (*Dhammapada* 5).

When Dame Julian of Norwich was shown in her *Revelations of Divine Love* that sin was behovable (necessary), but that all shall be well, and all manner of thing shall be well, she was being initiated into a supreme mystery. Without the constant fall from the high standards that God has implanted in us, we would never acknowledge the supremacy of those standards, and would certainly never attain them in the course of our life on earth. They would remain wonderful ethical ideals on which to meditate but without actually practising in the course of a day's sweat and toil.

Sin makes forgiveness possible, and forgiveness heralds the advent of the new man, who is no longer limited in vision by his deserts, privileges and rewards, but who moves in compassion to take on the burden of all created things.

Meditation

I thank you, O Lord, for the divine discontent deeply placed within my soul which will never let me be until I give myself wholly to your service.

12

Equanimity: the Precious Fruit of Suffering

The one who has emerged entire through the winnowing fire of suffering comes out changed and renewed. He has passed beyond dependence on things mortal and has attained a knowledge of the immortal Principle that lies at the root of his own being — which is also the immanent deity. He has passed beyond pleasure and pain to an inner centre where the peace of God is known. He is neither elated by success nor dejected by failure — as the world understands these two results of action, both of which are in fact illusions — but lives in the only fully substantial world, which is one of *union of all things in God.* The core of equanimity is well expressed in the *Bhagavadgita*: "To action alone hast thou a right and never at all to its fruits; let not the fruits of action be thy motive; neither let there be in thee any attachment to inaction" (2:47). In other words, the supreme act of man is to be attentive to God's will and do what is required of him. His reward is the eternal knowledge of God which far outstrips any material advantages that might accrue from it.

In the Parable of the Labourers in the Vineyard (Matthew 20:1–16), the tragedy of those who had laboured throughout the whole day was their blindness to the privilege and blessing of working in God's kingdom. That kingdom is every place in which we find ourselves and have the ability to use the gifts with which we have been endowed. Those who came late were much less fortunate, since they enjoyed the heavenly peace for a comparatively short time. But whosoever enters that kingdom gains the reward of eternal life when he puts away thoughts of recompense or demands of reward. The divine munificence is such that even the late-comer is not penalised except by his own tardiness in arriving to enjoy the divine company.

In the Parable of the Prodigal Son (Luke 15:11–32), the tragic figure is the dutiful, no doubt formally religious, older son who is unaware of his good fortune in sharing his father's estate, and this not through his merits but by virtue of his birth as a son of his father. His father reminds him of something so obvious that he had failed to notice it: "My boy, you are always with me, and everything I have is yours." The greater joy is to be able to welcome home a brother, who is every man in distress and disrepute, once dead and now come back to life, once lost and now found. Both the father and the returning son had come to this higher understanding of living in God's love as a result of pain: the father as if bereaved of a beloved son, and the son fallen into the despair of penury. When they came to each other again, each had grown from the natural possessiveness that men have for the things of this world to a breadth of self-giving that alone can participate in the divine kingdom. One hopes that the outraged suffering of the elder son, assuaged by the love of the other two, brought him into the kingdom of grace also.

In the blessed state of equanimity, which is called "holy indifference" in the Christian mystical tradition, one is in constant relationship with Him who is the eternal Father. The Buddhist teaching on non-attachment leads to this state of equanimity, but it requires the act of self-sacrifice to raise it from a mere technique of inner cleansing to a way of life that dedicates itself to the liberation of all sensual creatures from the thraldom of time to the expansiveness of eternity. The fruit of equanimity is purposeful, mindful action, the focus of which is God and not the fearful, self-centred person obsessed with the desire to achieve results in order to justify himself. Only when we are centred in the spirit can our actions be direct, harmonious, perfectly executed, and of wide benefit to others. The power of God the Holy Spirit works unimpeded and undisturbed through the person who is at peace in himself and in unitary consciousness with God. He no longer makes demands for himself, because he and the Father are united in will and are one in concern for the world.

Holy indifference means a state of acceptance of things as they are, including the results of one's actions, once they have been brought in faith to God. When Jesus, at the end of a terrible agony of doubt in mind and pain in body, finally prepares to give up His life, He says in what is traditionally accepted as His final utterance from the cross: "Father, into thy hands I commit my spirit" (Luke 23:46). This is an act of submission in complete faith; at this juncture He knows nothing of the resurrection ahead of Him. He has done what He set out to do, and although the result appears disastrous in terms of leading men to the kingdom of Heaven, He gives back to His Father what He had earlier been given, the divine spark. We know that this essence of God had already been glorified because of the wonderful work Jesus had done while on earth. We know that His physical body was to become resurrected into a body of pure spiritual light, universally available to those in all successive ages who call upon His name in faith, as He freely gave up His life as an offering of love to all who had been imprisoned in their own sinful existence. But He knew nothing of all this as He surveyed the tempestuous course of His brief ministry on earth. The terrible cry from the heart: "My God, my God, why hast thou forsaken me?" finds its conclusion in an acceptance of things as they are. He had done the deed as best as He was able; the judgement lay with the Father and the results were to be seen in the changed consciousness of all who had been brought into contact with Him.

When He was at the height of His ministry, He had prepared His disciples on three occasions for the final conflict, passion and rising again from the dead. But when He had to undergo these predicted events, His memory was occluded, a circumstance that, I believe, followed the terrible agony in the Garden of Gethsemane. At that encounter with the full weight of psychic destructiveness and evil, though He survived through the power of prayer, He was divested of the inner knowledge that so distinguished the triumphant part of His earlier work. He had to live through the last period as a diminished person in full identity with a diminished humanity, which is what we all are except in union with God. He made that union possible for all people by the supreme act of suffering with them, so that, in the depth of their own agony, they could be with God.

The triumph of the agony of suffering is that one enters a new realm in which there is neither pain nor pleasure, punishment nor reward, but only the peace of perfect knowledge of God. It is a strange and not unamusing paradox of the spiritual life that one enters into the divine kingdom only after one has parted with everything one had previously held dear, especially one's own reputation. Indeed, Jesus warns His disciples to be careful when people speak well of them for thus they spoke of the false prophets in the past. Only the person who has renounced himself completely can be God's prophet, for then he speaks from the authority of the Holy Spirit, untainted by personal prejudices and resentments. It is no wonder that the true prophet is tried in the white fire of affliction, and as his ministry proceeds, so does his faith increase in intensity. Even so great a prophet as Jeremiah had to learn this truth, which was the real answer to the impassioned dialogues he had had with God earlier in his ministry. It was said mockingly of Jesus on the cross: "He saved others, but he cannot save himself." The servant of God, who is the eternal suffering servant, has to pass beyond the polarities of health and illness, imprisonment and freedom, pain and pleasure, life and death, before he can know the way of eternity. Only then can he be the "way-shower" for those who follow him. Each of us has to recapitulate the life of a full person in Christ before we can enter the kingdom of God, but Christ is with us in our travail because He is the "first fruits of the harvest of the dead" (as St Paul writes in I Corinthians 15). He goes on to say: "As in Adam all men die, so in Christ all will be brought to life; but each in his own proper place; Christ the first fruits, and afterwards, at his coming, those who belong to Christ. Then comes the end, when He delivers up the kingdom to God the Father" (verses 22–24). The first fruits are first in a hierarchy of spiritual eminence, not of temporal succession, and those who belong to Christ are not those who say 'Lord, Lord', but those who do the will of God the Father (Matthew 7:21).

A state not unlike that of equanimity can be achieved after a long well-conducted retreat from the world in some situation of peace and beauty. The scales gradually drop from the eyes of the retreatant, and the clamant bustle of life's continual demands is slowly stilled amid the silence of nature. An even more prolonged state of holy indifference to the world's demands and rewards can follow a secluded life in an Eastern ashram. Many young people nowadays opt for such an experience and some spend years in this type of spiritual retreat. It would seem that equanimity can, after all, be attained in much more harmonious surroundings and by means of far less harrowing methods than the submergence of the personality in the dark river of suffering. Indeed, to some modern minds, this emphasis on the necessity for suffering as a way to the full attainment of spiritual mastery must seem overdone if not frankly morbid. But it must also be said that the even-tempered indifference to the outer flux of circumstances that one may acquire in a situation of retreat is a very precariously balanced state. If such a person were to return to the chaos and psychic havoc of the secular city, it is doubtful, to say the least, whether he would retain a calm façade, let alone a tranquil inner composure. Indeed, it is important to bring the retreatant firmly back to the worldly situation before he returns home, lest the contrast presents a temporarily unbearable shock to his nervous system. This is done by the experienced conductor giving his flock clear instructions about a disciplined prayer life, which should be augmented by their presence in a worshipping community. One has, as it were, to bring a little of the peace and dedication that one was given during the period of inner silence to the noise and bustle of the surrounding heedless world. Only then can the equanimity experienced in the silence be gradually realised in the life of active participation in the world's problems. Thus it is evident that the tranquillity one may experience in a quiet situation away from the demands of the busy, heedless world is a long distance from the holy indifference known to the saints of the world's great religious traditions. This is heralded by a change in the person's awareness of reality that follows the purifying effect of loss and suffering. The preliminary awareness of peace in a chosen retreat situation is not to be derided however; it is a way towards spiritual vision divested of the illusion of personal ownership. But it will become a permanent feature of the person's life only after much that he believed was important has been cut away by suffering, and he is left with only the pearl of great price within himself. This is the kingdom within, and it radiates an atmosphere of indifference to the world's judgements and a joyful recognition of the power of God in all situations.

Equanimity is a state in which one proceeds with the duties of one's calling in obedience to the ever-present voice of God. This speaks silently in the depths of one's being, but informs the will with purpose and the intellect with obedience and compassion. The voice of God never dominates the personality; it stands at the door of consciousness and knocks for admission. If God is consciously admitted to our lives, He does not take them over; on the contrary He shows Himself as an intimate friend. He is constantly available to support us and show us the way to liberation from the bondage of all earthly attachments, but He does not intrude to make His presence felt. Dame Julian of Norwich was amazed at the courtesy of our Lord: a courteous person respects the identity and integrity of the other individual, no matter how unimportant he may appear in the world's eyes. In the state of holy indifference, or non-attachment, one is released from all concerns save that of doing the will of God. And this is God's will: that all of us should grow to mature manhood, measured by nothing less than the full stature of Christ (Ephesians 4:13). We work as compatriots with God; without Him all our actions fail, while without us the world's glory does not unfold. As St Irenaeus put it: "The glory of God is a living man." Such a man was manifested in Jesus Christ, and we are to be like Him, since "God became man in order that man might become God", as St Athanasius saw in a flash of supreme intuition. Man's end is "theosis" or deification, an end prefigured in the Incarnation of Christ.

In this respect equanimity is very different from quietism, a heretical view of the relationship between God and man in which the human initiative is put in abeyance so that man may be the completely passive instrument of God. This aberrant spiritual approach occurs in many mystical groups who, while rightly submissive to divine grace, fail to give due weight to the positive contribution of the human will to God's work in the world. As Psalm 127 reminds us: "Unless the Lord builds the house, its builders will have toiled in vain. Unless the Lord keeps watch over a city, in vain the watchman stands on guard." But nevertheless it is the builder who provides the strength and patience by which the house is erected; it is the trustworthy watchman who stands on guard. Both God and man are essential for the work. The one without the other will achieve nothing. It is the divine courtesy that has given man his essential place in building the world, and God emphasises this human necessity categorically in the Incarnation of Christ. "Yet thou hast made him little less than a god, crowning him with glory and honour. Thou makest him master over all thy creatures; thou hast put everything under his feet" (Psalm 8:5–6)

It can be said with some irony that man is now in command of such unlimited physical resources that he may well destroy himself and all the creatures of this earth with nuclear energy, even within this century, unless he undergoes a radical spiritual change. Such a change may well be the fruit of a terrible humiliation and loss of life. What we call evil is often part of the experimentation of man in understanding the world and gaining inner mastery. A young child will pull out the wings of a living insect with little awareness of the distress he is causing that small creature. Only as he himself learns how it feels to be injured physically and hurt emotionally does he come to identify himself with all God's creatures. And in this life there seem to be some who are morally incapable of learning how to enter into another person's suffering. The vast span that separates the bestiality of a Hitler from the spirituality of a Gautama or a Jesus is one of the mysteries of creation. It certainly tells us that there is an extensive journey to be made by the individual human being before he can transcend the purely animal nature in which he is clothed and participate in the divine nature, from which he arose in the beginning as an unconscious, undifferentiated soul and to which He is to return as a vibrant, articulate spirit.

The fully alive man has entered on the way of non-attachment. This does not restrict itself only to material possessions or the opinions that other people might have of oneself. It also involves personal relationships. When Jesus asks, rhetorically, having been told that His mother and brothers are outside asking for Him: "Who is my mother? Who are my brothers?" and looks round at those who are sitting in the circle about Him, He answers His own question: "Here are my mother and brothers. Whoever does the will of God is my brother, my sister, my mother" (Mark 3:32–35). He is showing the true non-attachment that is the heart of equanimity. He is not diminishing His mother or brothers, whom He loves, but is raising up in love all those who love His Father. Eventually, in the time of His passion, He is able to love even those who hate Him and all He stands for. Love has to flow unrestricted even upon those who seem to be least worthy of love. Only by love can they be helped to attain the spiritual stature for which they too are destined. It is in this way that Jesus Himself grows in perfection, as we have already read in Hebrews 5:7–10. Of course, while we are alive there will always be some people who claim a special degree of affection; in the instance of Jesus it seems to have been Mary Magdalene and the beloved disciple John. But even then the resurrected Christ tells Mary of Magdala not to cling to Him, for she was evidently in the act of embracing Him once she recognised Him. In the divine realm there are no special favourites; conversely everyone there is part of a favoured community. On a more earthly level, the only real way of passing beyond the gaping chasm of bereavement is to see the face of the beloved in every person one meets in one's daily life. There is a very deep significance in the disciples' recognition of Jesus in the person of the stranger whom they met on the road to Emmaus. Indeed, He is in every stranger we meet once we have the courtesy and the love to open ourselves to that person and partake of his inner being. But this is a gift of the way of non-attachment. As God told Samuel in the affair of the choice of the young David as king of the Israelites: "The Lord does not see as man sees: men judge by appearances but the Lord judges by the heart" (I Samuel 16:7). Only when we are in a state of equanimity can we effect that higher judgement, for then we are attached to God and not to men.

To love a person means to give oneself unreservedly to him so that he may be as God intended him to be. If one makes any personal demands on that person, one's love is soon perverted through possessiveness to strangling selfishness. What begins as human love all too often ends in disillusionment and cynicism, because we feel we have been let down. It is only when we do not need the emotional support of the other person that we can love him even to the extent of giving up our life for him. This disinterestedness is the very heart of true service. If we are attached to the one we help by bonds of deep affection, our personal concern will tend to intrude in the work we are called to do. We will be constantly getting in the way of his growth into a full person, just as an over-solicitous, neurotically possessive parent can cripple the growth of his children into the independence that is a prerequisite for mature adulthood.

Non-attachment must, however, be contrasted with detachment. A detached person has a cold, clinical attitude towards the sufferings of other people. He will tend to see their sufferings simply as the way of retribution or of growth of that individual, and feel himself unconnected with them. A non-attached person, on the other hand, is always available to lend a helping hand and a sympathetic ear to anyone in distress. He helps to bear the burden, but does this in such a way that the victim of misfortune is strengthened in his path to become a better, more authentic human being. This is the way of Christ. "Come to me, all whose work is hard, whose load is heavy; and I will give you relief. Bend your necks to my yoke, and learn from me, for I am gentle and humble-hearted; and your souls will find relief. For my yoke is good to bear, my load is light" (Matthew 11:28–30). In fact, the load of Christ is the sin of the whole world, and it is beyond conception in its magnitude. But even this can be borne when we put the clamant ego on one side, moving beyond our own demands for recognition and recompense, and giving ourselves freely to God's service. This is how equanimity alone can bear the burdens of the world. In this blessed state we are assured of Christ's love and forgiveness and that we are of infinite value in His regard.

There is a reciprocal relationship between prayer and equanimity. It is not possible to enter the depths of contemplative prayer until one has set aside all personal demands and aspirations. On the other hand, the practice of God's presence in silent contemplation makes an attitude of non-attachment more available in everyday life. One starts one's prayer life in dialogue with God, making one's requests known to Him; the end of prayer is silent contemplation of the One beyond all names with these words in one's mind and on one's lips: "Thy will be done." This is equanimity, the supreme mystical

reality of personal integrity before the Almighty. It is perfectly
summed up in the famous prayer of Rabi'a, an early Sufi saint:
"O my Lord, if I worship Thee from fear of hell, burn me in
hell; and if I worship Thee from hope of paradise, exclude me
from paradise; but if I worship Thee for Thine own sake, then
withold not from me Thy eternal beauty." Indeed, the joy of
prayer is communion with God; all benefits that might follow
this communion pale into insignificance beside the peace of
God that passes human understanding. We have to bring this
communion with God into the world in which we give our
humble service so that a little of the peace of God may enter
into our personal relationships. From there the peace may
pervade the troubled psychic atmosphere of the world, and
gradually effect a change in the consciousness of all men, so
that, from being instruments of destruction and hatred, they
may emanate goodwill towards their neighbours. This is the
way of prayer that can alone save our generation from destruction. But it is only those who have passed beyond the
polarities of pleasure and pain, reward and punishment, good
and evil, that can be the agents of the new covenant between
God and man which Christ initiated by His sacrificial death.
Only the person who has passed triumphantly through the
refining fire of suffering can be a minister of healing for our
scarred, shattered world. He no longer speaks merely for
himself, but is a spokesman for all who have suffered and are
dispossessed. Through his purified soul shines the uncreated
light of God.

   In this blessed equanimity of spirit one can begin to enjoy
the world as it is. One discovers that its marvels are the things
of everyday life one so takes for granted in one's ceaseless
strife and anxiety that one misses them until it is almost too
late to appreciate them. One begins to feel the joyous activity
of a healthy body, the clean, purifying thrust of ice-cold water
on the tongue and palate, the invigorating air penetrating the
nostrils to the lungs within, and the heat of the sun playing on
the skin until it responds in warmth to the beneficence around

it. This is the peace that passes human understanding, the peace of Christ such as the world cannot give. It comes to those who have put themselves on one side so that they can give everything they have to life, the life of abundance. Having nothing they possess all things, needing nothing the world is theirs. They may be poor by human standards, but the riches within their spirit are inexhaustible. "You shall know the truth, and the truth will set you free," Jesus said to those who had believed Him (John 8:32). They unfortunately could see freedom only in terms of personal independence as opposed to national slavery. But until one has known the pain of servitude and has passed beyond the personal revolt that this of necessity engenders, one can never know the real freedom of the Spirit.

Freedom is ultimately an attitude of mind. One person may be free in spirit even when crippled, blind and destitute. Another may be in bondage even with enormous possessions of wealth, power and psychic gifts. The only reality is God, and those who are closest to the divine nature are closest to their own soul. These have been cleansed of the external dross that men in their ignorance esteem so much by the fire of God's love in the crucible of suffering. Indeed, one begins to see how complementary are the judgement and the love of God. The one purifies the soul while the other heals it. This reciprocal action is the inner meaning of growth. And growth is the one essential property of life. Life never ceases except inasmuch as it ends in union with God Whose Spirit is the Lord, the giver of life.

Rabi'a was once asked "Do you love God Almighty?" "Yes." "Do you hate the devil?" "My love of God," she answered, "leaves me no leisure to hate the devil. I saw the prophet in a dream. He said, 'O Rabi'a, do you love me?' I said 'O Apostle of God, who does not love thee? but love of God hath so absorbed me that neither love nor hate of any other thing remains in my heart.'" This quotation (taken from *A Literary History of the Arabs* by R A Nicholson) expresses the true meaning of love in equanimity. When one is centred on God, each person takes his own place in one's love. Hatred and fear, even of what is destructive and evil in the world, are stilled, and a radiance extends to embrace all creatures, whether here or in the psychic realms beyond mortal life. Even such calamities as personal loss and the death of those close to one are now seen in their eternal mode, as a part of the soul's journey to a knowledge of God. Pain gives way to joyous relief and resentment to divine thanksgiving. This is the final fruit of suffering endured with courage and transcended with faith.

Suffering is seen to be the probationary path to selfhood in God.

Meditation

The peace of God, that peace which passes all understanding and is of such a different order from the repose associated with the satisfaction of material craving, consists entirely in opening ourselves to His grace and knowing that all things work to good in eternity to those who love Him and give of themselves freely as a living sacrifice to their fellow creatures.

13

Taking up the Cross

The demands that Jesus made of those who wished to become disciples were very strict. "Anyone who wishes to become a follower of mine must leave self behind; he must take up his cross, and come with me. Whoever cares for his own safety is lost; but if a man will let himself be lost for my sake and for the Gospel, that man is safe. What does a man gain by winning the whole world at the cost of his true self? What can he give to buy that self back? If anyone is ashamed of me and mine in this wicked and godless age, the Son of Man will be ashamed of him, when he comes in the glory of his Father and of the holy angels" (Mark 8:34–38).

We do not *have* to seek a cross to bear nor do we *have* to make martyrs of ourselves. Indeed, we are taught in the Lord's Prayer to ask that we may *not* be brought to the test. People who expose themselves to unnecessary risks and dangers on behalf of God or what they believe is God's will, are usually found to be either fanatics or simply exhibitionists. They do not ring true. They tend to repel, rather than encourage honest seekers on the way to the knowledge of God. It is their ego that is in command, so that God is, in fact, the object of their self-centred enthusiasm rather than the subject of their aspiration. We all have, eventually, to face our special test or trial, but, through God's grace, we are shielded from this supreme moment until we are strong enough in the spirit to bear it.

The thoughts of Pascal are especially relevant in this respect. He writes: "It is tempting Me rather than proving yourself to think whether you would act well in some case that has not occurred: I shall act in you if it does." Even Jesus bore His supreme cross only at the end of His ministry when, as the writer of the Letter to the Hebrews puts it, He had learned obedience in the school of suffering and had offered up prayers and petitions, with loud cries and tears, to God who was able to deliver Him from the grave.

The cross we are all called on to bear is a defect in our own personality that prevents us from showing ourselves in full glory to the world. It is either some difficulty that has been with us since our birth, or else it is a wound inflicted upon us by our environment, so that we bear a permanent scar, either on the body, or even more pertinently, in the psyche for the remainder of our life on earth. It is strange to contemplate the paradox of the Creator who saw that all He had created was good, as the Genesis myth quite rightly states, and the seeds of creation that are so often aberrant and warped. Theologically this decline from initial perfection is interpreted as a result of man's fall from the divine kingdom by the selfish use of his will. But, as I have already stated, I believe all this was part of God's plan to enable man to attain divine knowledge as a responsible individual, so that he could play his part with God in the creation and maintenance of our world. Certainly, according to the mythological account of the Fall described in Genesis 3, God created both the tempting serpent, who was to become the most powerful symbol of the devil in man's life, and the tree in the middle of the garden, the tree of the knowledge of good and evil. One can hardly doubt that man would inevitably be tempted to master all mysteries according to his own will. The fall from God's kingdom is the birth into individual consciousness which is a necessary stage in the development of a full human being. It has been said with some wisdom by a psychoanalyst that evil is that which awaits transformation. Indeed, it may even be the transforming agent in God's economy. Life is openness, openness to oneself, to God, and to all the circumstances of life, to those which appear evil no less than to those that are good. The faith that saves is an attitude of openness to the fecundity of life's experiences, to the "givenness" of God. It does not require a theologically reasoned approach to the divine mystery so much as an availability to the healing power of the present moment. This is the sacrament of the present moment, that J. P. de Caussade speaks of in his spiritual classic, *Self-Abandonment to the Divine Providence*.

I have recently had my attention drawn to an observation in Sir Thomas Browne's *Religio Medici*: "In the most imperfect creatures — and such are everywhere where the power of the sun is — in these is the wisdom of His hand discovered." This view is complementary to an insight of R. W. Emerson in his *Essay on Compensation*: "There is a crack in everything God has made." These two thoughts deserve profound reflection. It is the imperfection of the creature, the crack in the finished product, that is the way to a knowledge of God in the life of that creature. The flaw might indeed be an example of God's turning a fallen world in its own very falling to its own best advantage. Perfection in human form would make one so god-like, at least in one's own estimation and in that of the foolish people who form the majority of the race, that one might feel no need for further exertions. To act as if one has arrived at perfection, or the full truth about life, is to approach dangerously near the stagnation of death. Paradoxically, only when one has died to this seductive delusion, does one start to live authentically again, and on a higher spiritual level. This thought adds a deeper dimension to the Parable of the Publican and the Pharisee.

The cross we have to bear is the signpost on the way we are to go to become full human beings. It is, in other words, our way of growth to self-mastery, and like all growth, it has its quota of pain. In the course of natural selection that is the heart of the process of evolution, the species that survives is the one that has triumphed over its difficulties by means of the development of some new characteristic that allows it to live more profitably in its environment. In a somewhat similar way, it is suffering that is the spur to scientific research which increases the knowledge and power of the human race. But whereas we believe that the development of a new characteristic in an animal is the result of a fortuitous, or random, genetic mutation that is inherited by the offspring to their natural advantage in an indifferent environment, it is in man's power through the gift of a brilliant mind to alter the environment, as well as his response to it, as a result of exploration, experimentation and the implementation of the results of his research. Where there is no pain there is no growth, but only a sleepy, rather irresponsible state in which people do as little as possible so as to avoid exertion or commitment to anything except their immediate comfort. Furthermore, it is in times of national suffering rather than during periods of prosperity that people come closest together. When all are in pain or in danger of extermination, they remember their common humanity and cease to look down on or exploit each other.

The cross we all have to bear can be likened to the yellow star of David that Jews were forced to wear during the Nazi occupation of Europe. It was a sign of discrimination, of ostracism, and of death. But it also had the character of distinction, perseverance and ultimate resurrection. The remarkable vision that Ezekiel had when he was shown the plain full of bones which were resurrected to full human stature as an immense living army (Ezekiel 37:1–10) is a symbol of the historical situation of this great people. In their human form they have been subjected to the full gamut of fate's vicissitudes — never powerful in number and yet never extinguished despite the frequent jealousy they have aroused in others — but each tragedy has been succeeded by a regeneration of a fresh remnant that has added its lustre to the world. Their contribution has been to the human mind and spirit. Two other great religions, Christianity and Islam, owe their existence to the abiding Hebrew witness to the sovereignty of God despite all temptations to turn from the invisible splendour and worship the idols contrived by man. And the achievements of the human mind in the realms of art, science and philosophy have been incalculably enriched by the Jewish contribution. Yet even this people with their ancient store of wisdom and their enormous enthusiasm for life are still only at the threshold of their true vocation: to be a nation of priests which will be a light to the whole world. This was revealed in their greatest representative, Jesus of Nazareth, and still awaits its implementation as a witness to all people. It certainly has, as yet, not been shown by any of the world's great religions, including the one that takes its name from Christ.

"Not everyone who calls me 'Lord, Lord' will enter the kingdom of heaven, but only those who do the will of my heavenly Father. When the day comes many will say to me 'Lord, Lord, did we not prophesy in your name, cast our devils in your name, and in your name perform many miracles?' Then I will tell them to their face: 'I never knew you; out of my sight, you and your wicked ways!' " (Matthew 7:21–23). The solution to this paradox lies in the attitude of those who proclaim the Lord's name. To return to the strict demands made by Christ, which I mentioned at the beginning of this chapter, it is said that anyone who is ashamed of Him or His, the same will Christ be ashamed of. In fact all life, and especially human life, is of Christ, and so the true Christian dare not turn his back on, let alone persecute or hurt, any creatures, especially human beings. It is of the accusation of cruelty that both the Semitic monotheistic religions that have arisen from the fundamental Jewish insight so often stand condemned. In the Hindu-Buddhist tradition there is, on the other hand, far too great an indifference to the plight of man as a social being, an attitude fostered by a metaphysic that regards the phenomenal world as little more than an insubstantial illusion which is to be transcended when the round of rebirth is extinguished in the bliss of Nirvana. It is exactly in this type of society that Western socially-orientated philosophies are so desperately needed, just as the Western world needs the understanding of non-attachment that comes from Eastern spiritual practice.

The cross that is our personal lot brings us to a full measure of our humanity, and when properly accepted, lifts us beyond the dual temptations of cruelty and indifference to the plight of our fellow creatures. To bear one's cross requires first of all the courage to acknowledge it in clear consciousness, and that without self-abhorrence or indeed any kind of adverse judgement. We are told by our Lord to "love our neighbour as ourselves"; this is indeed the second great commandment, and it follows the first even greater commandment which is to love God with all our being. In fact there is only One who can truly love us as we now stand — whether we be criminal or saint — and that is God, "unto whom all hearts are open, all desires known, and from whom no secrets are hidden". To love God requires the simple, yet very difficult, act of opening ourselves to God as we now are without either self-abasement or self-justification. Often this openness to God's love follows an experience of humiliating self-abasement which comes after we have behaved extremely badly, so much so as to have earned the contempt of all those around us. Deprived as it were of all human comfort in our self-inflicted misery, we are at last open to the reality of God's constant love towards us. And then a change takes place. What was previously hidden within us — so much so that we could hardly bear to face it in the clear light of consciousness — now becomes freely revealed to us as a lovable, if perverse, side of our own nature. And the corollary of this recognition of the whole of our personality, shadow side as well as spiritual aspiration, is that we can also begin to accept other people as they are, and love them for being what they are.

When we carry our cross in the full radiance of acceptance and love of it, we suddenly become aware of the presence of the risen Christ at our side. He is there, available to strengthen us in our travail, so that what was previously an intolerable burden now becomes an adventure into authentic living. The oft-quoted words, "Come to me, all whose work is hard, whose load is heavy; and I will give you relief", take on a new significance. And indeed the healing power of the Holy Spirit gradually transforms the earthly cross into a radiant cross of light in which dwells the risen Lord. Our wounds (to quote Dame Julian of Norwich again) have become worships, and we can be an instrument of God's healing power to all those in a similar distress.

It is furthermore in taking up our cross in courage and faith that we leave self behind. The self that is left behind is the dominating ego which likes to project a favourable image of oneself on to the world. When the depths of the personality are revealed by the cross that is borne, the ego is displaced from its dominant position to a secondary serving role by the true self, or soul, which is energised through its spirit by the Holy Spirit. It comes about therefore, that, if we follow Christ in honest acceptance of our full nature, the ego is gradually transfigured by the authentic self within, and we begin to function consciously at this level of identity ("I and the Father are one" John 10:30). The safety of the ego is as evanescent as is our mortal life; when we relinquish that safety for God's service, we discover a principle within us that survives the death of the body, because it is immortal. This is the true self with its spiritual centre. To know this true self is incomparably better than winning the whole world; this attainment too is fleeting and transitory, whereas the self within is eternal. Not all the world's riches can buy it back, since it is of God. Only heart-felt penance can restore the self to its place of centrality in a sinner's personality: even the Prodigal Son came to himself only when he had been brought to abject poverty and had lost everything he possessed.

A strong, yet unnecessary, ingredient in the sufferings we have to undergo is the tendency to compare ourselves with other people. This temptation is especially strong when one has to bear the type of cross that prevents one functioning freely in the society of the worldly ones. It is hurtful to compare the apparent happiness and success of one's peers with one's own manifest inadequacies and failures. To this pain is often added a fear that God is punishing one for one's sins; the distress that all these misconceptions are liable to engender can mount up to a black despair. How little one knows of what is happening in someone else's inner life! How seldom do we see the feet of clay on which a deceptively impressive person is supported! It is only in coming to terms with the full range of our own personality that we can start to know our fellow creatures for what they are. At last we begin to see the person instead of standing in rapt awe before an image of him that we ourselves have fashioned. Conversely, we stand in much greater respect of the common people around us whom we had previously dismissed as of little account. The widow who gave her tiny contribution to the temple treasury was commended by Christ as giving more than any of the others, including the rich who had given large sums. For they had more than enough left over for their subsistence and comfort, while she, with less than enough, had given all she had to live on (Mark 12:41–44).

In everyday life we are like sleep-walkers, oblivious of our benefits. We simply do not realise how privileged we are until we have allowed our cross to take us down into the hell where our brothers also live. As our cross is glorified and transfigured by Christ into something beautiful for God, so we may play our part in transfiguring the sordid society from which we ourselves gained our sustenance in earlier days. It is indeed in this way that social action becomes practical and inevitable: the spur is deep compassion born of shared suffering and not glib political and economic experimentations in which individuals are lumped together as "the masses" to be manipulated according to the power drives of ego-centred theorists. These are, of course, often well-intentioned enough in their desire to reform society, but they will inevitably work from the head rather than from the whole person until they too have been tried and refined in the furnace of suffering. One cannot really help "the masses" until one knows oneself to be a part of them, and remains a part of them throughout one's life. As soon as one starts to manipulate and organise others, one sets oneself apart from them in a superior position, and at once despotism rears its baneful head. The ego — our old Adam — has to be renewed in Christ before it may be one with the true self within. Only then can it be an agent of healing for the whole world.

Another cross many of us are called on to bear is the burden of unpleasant experiences in our childhood that leave psychological scars which prevent us living to our full potential. Not only is there a crack in our own personality, but it also extends into the society in which we were reared and into those who have had responsibility for our welfare. Man's inhumanity to man is often the result of deep inner deprivation which shows itself in such anti-social attitudes as anger, jealousy, race and religious hatred, and a desire for the destruction of all that is beautiful and noble. What the deprived person cannot attain, he wishes to destroy in others, and he is filled with malice against those who are happy and prosperous. He attributes underhand dealing to those who do well for themselves, especially if they are strangers. The pain that accrues from the injustice that men suffer as part of their social heritage can bite very deep, and in itself it eloquently testifies to the indivisible membership we all inherit in the full body of mankind.

These social and psychological disabilities are in part the special preserve of those who specialise in the social sciences and psychotherapy. But in the end the victim himself has to accept his afflictions as his particular cross to be borne among the vast army of struggling human beings. When we have finally, after much pain and recrimination, ceased to wage a continual war against the injustice of our lot — as Job did to his irritating comforters — and have come to the greater wisdom of accepting it as our contribution to bearing the collective sin of the world, only then can we move from destructive self-pity to a positive attitude in which we are able to use our particular experience for the benefit of other afflicted people. There are indeed two fundamental approaches to the suffering which is an inherent part of the life that we have been given by God's grace. We can either opt out of life by means of a variety of self-destructive manoeuvres ranging from drug addiction and crime to suicide, or else we can persist in the faith that there is a deeper meaning to the apparently purposeless flow of our existence. In this faith we will never give up the struggle until we have been granted a blessing from our adversary comparable to that exacted by Jacob from the angel of the Lord who contended with him.

Destructive gestures do not solve the problems of life; they merely extend them into the future, either of our present life or else into the life beyond death. It would be insensitive to condemn a destructive choice out of hand, because suffering is often too deep for any casual observer to fathom. But if one has the courage to persist, a present blessing will show itself: the ability to see life in its eternal mode and to know God as Father. As I have already indicated, these gifts are the fruit of terrible suffering that has been borne patiently and with courage. Only the one who has attained this knowledge can be of help to others. To be constantly available as a source of help to one's fellows is the greatest privilege one can know. Those who have survived ill-treatment and injustice as integrated people are special agents of God. They bear in their deeper psyche the authentic marks by which Thomas knew the risen Lord — the marks of the nails on His hands and the mark on His side where the soldiers stabbed the body with a lance, and from which blood and water flowed.

As the cross of life is held aloft to God in submissive triumph, so the memories of the past are renewed, reconsidered, and eventually healed. St Paul says: "It is not to be thought that I have already achieved all this (knowing Christ and arriving at the resurrection from the dead). I have not yet reached perfection, but I press on, hoping to take hold of that for which Christ once took hold of me. My friends, I do not reckon myself to have got hold of it yet. All I can say is this:

forgetting what is behind me, and reaching out for that which lies ahead, I press towards the goal to win the prize which is God's call to the life above, in Christ Jesus" (Philippians 3:12–14). This forgetting of the past does not mean a failure of memory, a state of amnesia. It would be a great loss if we were ever to relinquish the inner benefits of a past experience, no matter how terrible it was at the time. We learn more through our mistakes, our pains and our trials than we do from the occasional moments of triumph and ecstasy. What has to be lived through and healed is the emotional charge of our past history, that feeling of depression, fear, resentment or hatred, as the case may be, that accompanies painful memories. These emotional responses enter our consciousness and muddy the clear waters of our perception when we are confronted with a situation that evokes a strong past association. They poison all promising new relationships with people in the present; they insinuate themselves in the cheerful repose of everyday living so that we become irritable and distrustful; they destroy the inner peace that comes after a glorious aesthetic experience. Only when the emotional charge of the painful past has been transmuted into a feeling of thanksgiving for what we have been enabled to achieve and learn from it for the benefit of the whole human race, can we forget what is behind us and look in eager anticipation to what lies ahead. It is Christ who enters the memories of the past and redeems them from the bondage of regret to the glorious splendour of universal compassion. We do not need to contrive His entry into the inner room which is our true self; we simply have to open ourselves to His unseen presence, for He stands perpetually at the door knocking for admisson. When He had taken supper for the last time with His disciples, He gave them bread to eat and wine to drink that He had blessed. He consecrated the common elements of the earth so that they assumed an eternal role as His body and blood. "Do this as a memorial to me." Whenever we remember what He did for us and move beyond our groans of self-centred pity to embrace the whole world's pain, He enters our lives, redeeming the past and leading us in hope to our future work. For this transmutation of the memories of the past to occur, three requirements are necessary: a conscious awareness of the cross we have to bear and a presentation of it to God, work for our fellow men, and ceaseless prayer.

Our memories are healed as we experience the forgiveness of our sins, and we in turn are able to receive those who injured us as brothers. It is in this way that the radical demands of the Sermon on the Mount can be fulfilled. "Love your enemies and pray for your persecutors; only so can you be children of your heavenly Father, who makes His sun rise on good and bad alike and sends rain on the honest and the dishonest" (Matthew 5:44–45).

Meditation

That aspect of my character of which I am most deeply ashamed is, when confronted with courage and humility, my way of most intimate approach to the weakness of my brothers. Once I have learnt to love myself in all my parts, I find that I am also in love with all life. But first I must give of myself to God, who makes me infinitely lovable by infusing me with His love. Then my wound becomes an object of worship, just as the precious wounds of the crucified Christ were the way of Thomas knowing Him when He returned in His spiritual body.

14

Retribution and Suffering: the Significance of Atonement

There is a strong association between impure conduct and misfortune. Indeed this theme runs through most of the Old Testament; Israel's frequent apostasies, starting from the period in the wilderness under the leadership of Moses and proceeding to the Maccabean era and beyond, are blamed for national misfortune, whereas times of enlightened rulership under the three totally beneficent kings — David, Hezekiah and Josiah — are accompanied by revival and resurgence. In castigating the nation for its gross idolatry, Hosea writes: "Israel sows the wind and reaps the whirlwind; there are no heads on the standing corn, it yields no grain; and if it yielded any, strangers would swallow it up" (Hosea 8: 7–8). St Paul continues this theme: "Make no mistake about this: God is not to be fooled; a man reaps what he sows. If he sows seed in the field of his lower nature, he will reap from it a harvest of corruption, but if he sows in the field of the spirit, the spirit will bring him a harvest of eternal life" (Galatians 6:7–9).

As it often appears that the unjust do not seem to come to grave misfortune before they die, a view appears later in the Old Testament, and especially in the Apocrypha (in the Books of Wisdom and II Maccabees) that this life is the precursor of a larger life beyond death in which a final assessment of past actions will be made and an appropriate sentence passed. This assessment may be not so much one of eternal punishment or reward as one of a gradual ascent to spiritual awareness in an intermediate, purgatorial state that may involve the true self experiencing many different modes of existence. The idea of an intermediate state after death and the propriety of prayers for the dead is stated in II Maccabees 12:38–45. In this passage it is described how certain Jews who were killed in a battle in

which Israel was victorious, were found to have carried amulets
sacred to the idols of Jamnia, objects forbidden to the Jews
by the Law. Their deaths in battle were attributed to their
idolatry. The people praised the work of the Lord and, turning
to prayer, asked that the sin of the fallen might be blotted out.
As the writer notes, had they not been expecting the fallen to
rise again, it would have been both foolish and superfluous to
pray for them.

In the religion of ancient Greece and in the traditions of
Hinduism and Buddhism, it is believed that the essence of the
person, the true self, pre-exists the mortal being with which it
is associated. Likewise it proceeds with its journey, that ends
in its absorption into the Absolute, after the body dies. Some
accept that this journey entails rebirth in a series of human
bodies, an hypothesis called "reincarnation". Others believe
that the process of life beyond death occurs in other dimensions
rather than our limited planet, and the term "rebirth" would
seem more apposite than reincarnation. It is, of course, possible that rebirth into other modes of reality and reincarnation
are alternative parts of the soul's journey to full development
in the world beyond physical death. Despite much interesting
psychical research into the matter of survival, we can give no
certain proof of life beyond death, let alone details of the
process. In the end, it is the intimations that come to the
person directly that are most likely to guide him into the hazy
area of psychical knowledge in which he can discern trends in
the afterlife.

Personally I am not altogether sorry that there is as yet no
scientifically acceptable proof of survival. I do not think we
deserve it in our present state of spiritual awareness. In the
Parable of the Rich Man and Lazarus (Luke 16:19–31), the
wealthy one was told, as he languished in hell, that his five
brothers would not accept the reality of the afterlife and the
suffering that accrued from an ill-spent life on earth even if
someone from the dead visited them. Only those who listened
and obeyed the Law and the prophets could have this

knowledge. While one must have the most serious reservations about the harsh, irrevocable judgement portrayed in this parable, which denies the mercy of God to a chastened and potentially repentant sinner, on the question about an understanding of conditions beyond the grave the parable is soundly based. Profound spiritual knowledge can be given only to those who have led spiritual lives. One cannot gain the deepest knowledge second-hand from books, because the teaching does not penetrate until it resonates with the depths of one's own being. Only then is it understood and accepted. "Deep calls to deep in the roar of thy cataracts, and all thy waves, all thy breakers pass over me" (Psalm 42:7).

The acceptance of life's continuation beyond the death of its physical vehicle is crucial to our deeper understanding of suffering and its effect in building the person's soul structure. As St Paul puts it: "If it is for this life only that Christ has given us hope, we are of all men the most to be pitied" (I Corinthians 15:19); indeed the whole of I Corinthians 15 is a remarkable dissertation on the importance and meaning of survival in terms of the resurrection of the body. One thing is apparent: even those who live to a ripe old age and have spiritual understanding know how little they have achieved on the level of inner sanctification at the time of their death. We fail in love day after day, and the higher the degree of our spiritual understanding the more tragically aware are we of our lack of love to those less fortunate than we are. Without survival of death, there could be no growth of the person into something of the measure of a fully grown son of God.

How much of our present suffering is due to the misdeeds we committed in the past? Is suffering the direct result of sin, whether personal or communal? And if there is a direct relationship between past sin and present pain, can the past extend into a previous mode of existence before the present life? In the Hindu and Buddhist traditions, the concept of "karma" is very important. In itself this word simply means "action", but when used metaphysically it alludes to the moral law of cause and effect. In this respect the law of karma is unquestionable. St Paul's statement, quoted at the beginning of this chapter about a man reaping what he sows, is an excellent illustration of this law. Jesus likewise says: "For as you judge others, so you will yourselves be judged, and whatever measure you deal out to others will be dealt back to you" (Matthew 7:1–2).

That a great deal of our suffering is the direct result of bad actions in the years behind us is obvious to anyone with medical knowledge. Cigarette smoking is now known to be an important factor in the causation of a number of very unpleasant, lethal disorders, ranging from destructive lung disease and blockage of the arteries to the heart to a variety of malignant tumours. The gluttonous eating habits of those who live in privileged societies bring their harvest of circulatory, digestive and joint disorders later on in life, whereas the malnutrition of those who inhabit the underdeveloped countries of the world leads to the premature death of large numbers of people. And our present permissive attitude to personal morality is not without due retribution in its toll of venereal disease, drug abuse, and emotional breakdown. There is a relationship between states of psychological disturbance and bodily ill-health, although the pattern tends to vary according to the individual; no categorical correlation between mental states and physical illness is entirely accurate because the personal response to outer circumstances varies so widely. In the same way unassuaged guilt for wrongful action in the past will eventually demolish the physical and mental health of the sinner until he confesses his past misdeeds to God and seeks absolution. But many people are so insensitive to the feelings of others and so obtuse morally that they do not realise how their selfishness is cutting them off from full communion with their fellows and separating them from the power of the Holy Spirit, who gives us life and brings us to the full fruition of our personality. The moral law is contravened at our peril; for a long time we may seem to escape unnoticed, but in due course the finger of Nemesis points directly at us, and then suffering begins.

Jesus told the story, in Luke 12:17–21, of a rich man whose land yielded heavy crops. He had so much produce that he did not know what to do with it. In the end he decided to build large storehouses in which to contain all his goods. Then he said to himself: "Man, you have plenty of good things laid by, enough for many years: take life easy, eat, drink and enjoy yourself." But God said to him: "You fool, this very night you must surrender your life; you have made your money — who will get it now?" This is the way of the man who amasses wealth for himself and remains a pauper in the sight of God. This parable does not necessarily imply the physical death of the rich man, so much as the death of his past life and a descent into suffering that may be caused by ill-health, mental breakdown or a wider national disaster that brings to nothing all his private schemes of self-aggrandisement.

That much suffering is a direct retribution for selfish actions in the past cannot be denied. And even if we personally have lived cleanly and with charity to others, we cannot escape the collective guilt that is part of the social class to which we belong or the society in which we flourish. The rich have, at least since biblical times, ground the faces of the poor in the dust, just as until very recently those who were born fair-skinned have had an enormous social and economic advantage over their dark-skinned brothers. The present escalating unrest and violence in the world, which may well presage the total annihilation of the human race unless there is a radical change in our attitude to life and the values by which we work together, is the result of centuries of social and economic injustice. On the other hand, the great religious insights of the past have all too often been used simply to sustain a self-perpetuating establishment rather than being the way of mankind's advancement towards a full realisation of the divine image in which it has been fashioned. In our world no one who has lived to an adult age can be considered totally innocent; we all bear the sins of the past (including that of distant ages before our own birth), and only when we enter into the world's travail can we begin to heal the many wounds of the past. In this we proclaim the leadership of Christ, by whom the process of redemption was started. But we too have to play our part; suffering is both our contribution and our way towards proficiency in healing other people.

It is evident that there are two levels of suffering, the *retributive* and the *redemptive*. The first level is that undergone by the unawakened person whose frequent misdemeanours transgress the moral law of cause and effect — the principle of karma. When that person has woken up to his responsibility, he ceases to amass adverse karma as he starts to live according to the spiritual law instead of by thoughtless selfishness. But his sufferings do not cease; they may indeed become more intense as he acts in union with Christ to save the lost sheep of humanity. Then, however, his suffering assumes a redemptive character. Although the pain does not diminish, it is no longer submitted to with the blind incomprehension of an animal being goaded by a brutal overseer. The awakened person begins to see the deeper significance of his travail, so that a sense of purpose informs his suffering. This is, in fact, simply an application of a principle repeatedly stressed in these pages: as one grows in spirituality through the refining fire of suffering, so the ego is displaced from its customary seat of dominance to its proper place of service on behalf of the whole person. No wonder Jesus told His disciples who were vying with each other for the best places at the heavenly banquet: 'Among you, whoever wants to be great must be your servant, and whoever wants to be first must be the willing slave of all. For even the son of Man did not come to be served but to serve and to give up his life as a ransom for many" (Mark 10:43–45). This text, which has already been quoted, is especially apposite to the relationship between the ego, by which we show ourselves in the world, and the whole personality. In the end, as we have seen, the ego must coincide with the self; then the person and God are indeed working in unity together.

In redemptive suffering the person in travail has passed beyond outraged complaints and comforting thoughts of future recompense, even in the life beyond death, to a state of acceptance of things as they now are. His mind has been lifted beyond the pangs of the body to the suffering of mankind. He has entered the transpersonal life, and is one with his meanest brother as well as with the crucified Christ, who, as Pascal reminds us, will be in agony until the end of the world. He is crucified afresh whenever men behave with cruelty to each other. It is the way of spiritual growth to move from mere consciousness of the self to participation in the consciousness of all mankind, and finally of the whole creation. In mystical illumination this apparently impossible identification is glimpsed, albeit for only a fleeting moment. But what is revealed in telescopic compression to the mystic has to be brought down to earth and imparted to the brethren. "See that you work to the design which you were shown on the mountain" (Exodus 25:40).

This is a deeper understanding of the Atonement wrought by Christ. It is our privilege as we enter the fully spiritual path to participate, however humbly, in that great act of renunciation by which the world was led from heedless disintegration to spiritual aspiration. For God was in Christ reconciling the world to himself (II Corinthians 5:19). He spent himself even to death so that his little brothers might be lifted out of the chasm of darkness in which they had stumbled for so long and enter into the light of a new day. It is, to quote again from St Paul's Letter to the Colossians, our way of helping to complete in our poor human flesh the full tale of Christ's afflictions still to be endured, for the sake of his body which is the church (1:24). And that church is supra-denominational — it embraces all mankind, indeed the whole cosmos. In Him our sinful nature is redeemed and, to quote Jude 24, He can keep us from falling and set us in the presence of his Father's glory, jubilant and above reproach. The fruit of this healing of our sinful nature is that we emerge as re-created people, able to do God's work and participate in the spiritualisation, or divinisation, of the world.

But how do the sufferings of little children come into this scheme of retribution and redemption? They are too young to have been contaminated by lust and sin, and they can hardly be accused of participating, however unwittingly, in the selfishness of the society into which they were born. It is in this context of children's suffering that the hypotheses of pre-existence and rebirth are particulary attractive. Many appear to die too early to have any understanding of God's love or Christ's sacrifice on behalf of His fellow men. As I have already stated, all discussions about a past or future life are purely tentative inasmuch as the definitive scientific proof still eludes us. It is our own inner psychic awareness that is the best available instrument for exploring the shadow realms beyond physical existence. There are some people who claim to remember events that occurred before they were born, and the memories of small children have on occasion been found to tally with past events of whose existence they could not possibly have learned from their parents or others in their vicinity. At present there is considerable controversy as to the significance of these undoubtedly veridical childhood reminiscences. Are they really memory traces of a past life or is the child being obsessed by the personality of someone who has died recently? At present there is no way of distinguishing categorically between these two possibilities, but one fact has been established by psychical research: the existence of a mobile centre of consciousness that is not apparently limited by the situation of the physical body, but can travel extensively in other realms of existence and bring back information that can on occasions be confirmed. Mind and body do appear to be separate functions of a single person, certainly working together in the closest collaboration through the agency of the brain, and yet capable of absolute dissociation.

It is this finding that makes survival of death an intellectually acceptable, as well as a morally desirable, hypothesis and also sheds some light on theories of pre-existence, rebirth and reincarnation. One of the most fertile areas of mutual enrichment by the great religious traditions of the world is in this very field of human destiny. The Eastern traditions with their acceptance of rebirth have something to add to the Catholic purgatorial scheme. Above all the Christian understanding of the Atonement wrought by Jesus on the cross of man's affliction contributes a new dimension to the growth of the personality in the life of the world to come. We need desperately to learn from the insights of each other, and that in humility, not with the arrogant desire of proving others wrong that we may be seen to have possession of the whole truth. As is so often the case, each of the world's great religious traditions witnesses to particular truths that are not stressed elsewhere, while in other matters the tradition seems peculiarly blind to difficulties or obtuse to problems that are the basis of the strivings of those from other backgrounds. Speaking personally, I find the hypothesis of rebirth intellectually acceptable and morally satisfying; on whether it follows a reincarnational sequence invariably, sometimes, occasionally, or never, I do not venture an opinion. In any case this is a mere detail of a wider, more glorious process of spiritual advancement — to participate fully in the risen life of Christ.

The Christian will have some reserve about accepting a sequence of rebirth as I have outlined. For instance the text, "And it is the lot of men to die once, and after death comes judgement, so Christ was offered once to bear the burden of men's sins, and will appear a second time, sin done away, to bring salvation to those who are watching for Him" (Hebrews 9:27–28), seems to deny the possibility of more than one death. I personally would accept this statement on its face value as describing the death that we all have to undergo in this world with the subsequent judgement (however we may conceive this) in the after-life. I do not see that it rules out the possibility of the person's further birth into new realms of consciousness. Jesus Himself tells Nicodemus that we must be born again even in this life before we can see the kingdom of God (and Holy Baptism is a sacramental demonstration of this truth). Death as we understand it is, I am convinced, not a once-for-all event.

When a little child suffers a fatal illness, or is born severely deformed in body or mind so that it can never live a normal life or attain that degree of mental proficiency that is necessary to understand spiritual truths, it is often felt that its conception was a mistake. Indeed, there is a growing tendency in "advanced" societies to thwart the birth of children known to bear a defect by inducing an abortion early in the mother's pregnancy. The moral issues involved in this procedure are themselves agonising to those of us who see life as something more than mere bodily survival but who, at the same time, acknowledge the sanctity of the inner self of even the most defective person. By considering the deeper meaning of this type of tragedy we may come to a more soundly based way of dealing with it.

The first point to be made is that nothing that happens to us is a mere chance; there are no fortuitous events in the spiritual world. What appears to be a blind stroke of misfortune is also a golden opportunity for the one who is awake to the germ of a new possibility to grow into something of a better person than he was before the crucial event. In the ministry of Jesus there are two events that evoke teaching from Him on these lines. The first, which we have already noted, comes in Luke 13:1–5 and concerns Galileans who had been sacrificed by Pilate and people who were killed when a tower fell on them. Jesus told those around him that the victims were no greater sinners than those who had been spared, but that their fate was a warning to the survivors to repent. From this we learn that there is a greater significance to any life than that which concerns the individual to whom it belongs. In the oft-quoted words of John Donne: "No man is an island, entire of itself" and again "Any man's death diminishes me because I am involved in mankind; and therefore never send to know for whom the bell tolls; it tolls for thee." The defective child is a constant challenge to its parents and those who attend it; they can either reject it and become increasingly embittered against life, or else the springs of love may issue from a heart that was previously hard and demanding. As the heart softens, so the person begins to live with that abundance which Jesus came to proclaim and demonstrate in His own life. We have to learn to love a living being for what he is in himself, a child of God, and not for what that child may become or what we may gain from his later development and proficiency. This is a hard lesson. Furthermore, it may be that the defective child is an advanced soul who has come into the world in the greatest humility to teach those around it some vital lessons about love.

The other event that evoked important teaching from Jesus about the deeper issues of apparently meaningless suffering was the occasion, described in the ninth chapter of John's Gospel, when He healed a man blind since birth. His disciples wondered whose sin lay at the root of the man's blindness, his parents' or his own. Jesus denied, in this particular case, either suggestion. He said the man was born blind so that God's power might be displayed in curing him. Again there is communal involvement in both the man's affliction and his cure; he becomes a symbol of God's healing power and a manifestation of God's grace to many people. It is ironic that he, when questioned exhaustively by the religious authorities, said: "All I know is this: once I was blind, now I can see," whereas they, though normally sighted, remained spiritually blind. The healed man, on the other hand, gained physical and spiritual vision. His suffering had indeed been a blessing, even to him, for it had made him a witness as well as a testimony to God's love.

The ultimate answer to suffering, whether in adults or in the young, is not so much its antecedents as its results in the life of the person and the community. In other words, it is more important for us to learn the lessons that the affliction has brought in its wake than to spend endless time pondering its possible cause, whether in this life or in a postulated previous existence. One has known far too many people imbued with the philosophy of previous lives and accruing karma who claim to know the past dispositions that have led to the present circumstances and yet who remain painfully undeveloped spiritually. Their ego dwells on the romance of the past and remains as dominant as ever. The value of accepting a past history of the soul, one that precedes its present incarnation, is that it puts suffering in a wider perspective of time, and sees life as a series of lessons, or initiations, into greater sanctity. Indeed, when one meditates on the wonderful Book of Job, one sees that he was being initiated into a new way of life in which he no longer glimpsed God from afar, and tried to appease His wrath by suitable sacrifices lest misfortune should assail him and his family. Instead, he was given the privilege of knowing God directly and contemplating the mighty works of the Creator. And it is noteworthy that it was Satan, the adversary and accuser, who is the personified power of evil, that was the agent of initiation under the protective power of God.

Karma is in fact retribution only to the undeveloped person. He has to learn the same lesson time and time again until he passes life's primary examinations. Eventually he may graduate to a higher class when the ego is the servant of his soul and not its master. When he becomes a full human being, he plays his part in bearing the world's karma and he starts to redeem it in the presence of the One who bore the sins of the whole world and demonstrated the process of redemption and transfiguration. The risen Lord works ceaselessly towards the healing of the whole cosmos. It comes about that the karmic retribution of the unenlightened unfolds into the karmic opportunity of the fully awakened. The round of rebirth ceases to be simply a way of self-improvement ending in a final state of absorption into the Absolute, but becomes instead the vehicle of healing of all the world's suffering, until all creation enters transfigured into the divine presence. This to me is the essential contribution of the Atonement of Christ when one has entered into the undemanding love of Christ.

To my mind, the distinctive Christian contribution to the scheme of rebirth is the helping hand offered to all mankind by the risen Christ, who has atoned for the world's sins "by His one oblation of Himself once offered". He receives even the greatest sinner both now and after death, as soon as that person has had the humility and honesty to confront his own wretchedness and to confess it to God without flinching and without self-justification. Then Christ, like the father of the Prodigal Son runs to meet the sinner, takes him in His ever-lasting arms and embraces him in His unreserved love. The love of God removes the selfishness of remorse from the sinner, for it replaces it with such a love for the sinner's brothers, who are all mankind and indeed all created things, that he starts to lead a new life from that moment onwards and to do all he can to put right what he had previously done wrong.

In other words Christ redeems karma, the moral law of cause and effect. We have still to work out our own salvation and put our own house in order, but every experience in the future, no matter how forbidding it may seem on the surface, is now seen to be invested with new possibilities, for He is with us, and we are aware of His rod and staff comforting us, even when we traverse the valley of the shadow of death. Thus the law of cause and effect becomes the law of spiritual growth into the knowledge of the love of God.

Meditation

God's nature is always to have mercy on the sinner who is in all of us. We have only to ask His forgiveness to receive His absolution. We may emerge chastened by our sufferings, but God has given us a mind with which to reflect on the past, and a will to exert to better purpose in the future. Once we have had the courtesy to listen to what life is telling us, we are led in guided steps to the One Who gave up His life as a ransom for many. The end of suffering courageously borne is growth of the person into something of the nature of Christ, Who until then was merely a seed deeply planted in the soul and was awaiting germination to become the tree of life.

15

The Path to Wholeness

Since suffering is the inevitable path to self-mastery and service to others, it could well be argued that those who are in travail are best left to their own devices. Outside interference could impede the spiritual growth of the one in difficulties. Some votaries of the reincarnation hypothesis refrain from actively helping those in distress in the belief that these people are discharging an accumulated karmic debt from a previous ill-spent life through their sufferings in this one. This is indeed one of the baneful results of an unbalanced acceptance of rebirth and karma without the modifying factor of God's love and the atoning sacrifice made by Jesus Christ.

Extreme and unacceptable as these views are, they do nevertheless stress one aspect of suffering that is usually forgotten in our sentimental, sensationalised world: *it is a way of growth into a full human being, and it is interrupted at the peril of both the victim and the agent of healing.* Until one has claimed a blessing from one's pain, one cannot be freed from it, no matter how much the sensation be annulled by drugs or a charismatic healing gift. Once we, like our spiritual forefather Jacob, have obtained the blessing, we move forward, as if in a ceremony of initiation, to a greater knowledge of God and an augmented capacity to help those in need around us. The stern writer of the Letter to the Hebrews expresses this need for God's disciplinary rod thus: "In your struggle against sin, you have not yet resisted to the point of shedding your blood (as Christ did). You have forgotten the text of Scripture (Proverbs 3:11–12) which addresses you as sons and appeals to you in these words: 'My son, do not think lightly of the Lord's discipline, nor lose heart when he corrects you, for the Lord disciplines those whom he loves; he lays the rod on every son whom he acknowledges.' You must endure it as a discipline: God is treating you as sons. Can anyone be a son, who is not disciplined by his father?" (Hebrews 12:4–8).

Another important teaching about the way to wholeness is contained in Jesus' description, in Matthew 12:43–45, of the unclean spirit who leaves a man and wanders over the deserts seeking a resting-place. Finding none, it returns and finds the house unoccupied, swept clean and tidy. Off it goes to collect seven other spirits, more wicked than itself, and they all come in and settle down, so that, in the end, the man's plight is worse than before. Through this warning we can learn that a removal of some superficial difficulty or pain may not necessarily help the sufferer in his future life. If he is not at the same time changed inwardly so as to prove inhospitable to the invading powers of chaos and disintegration, he will more than likely be the victim of even worse disorder in the future. And the spirits are not necessarily obsessing psychic entities; they may even more probably show themselves in the form of physical diseases, moral lapses that lead to a breakdown in family relationships, and national disasters in which the person has played his part in endangering the solidarity of his own community. In fact there is the closest connection between inner states of malaise and the psychic milieu in which the deeper part of the mind functions, being as it is, in communion with the powers of darkness and light. All this is of the greatest importance both with regard to the deeper springs of suffering and to the efficacy of intercessory prayer, especially for the dead. One principle does stand out quite clearly: *wholeness does not consist in removing a present source of travail; it demands a complete transformation of the person's attitude to life, which in turn is an outward sign of a transfigured personality.* Suffering is the agent of transfiguration, and it will continue, in one form or another, until the person is changed into something of a son of God. As St Paul says, "Circumcision is nothing; uncircumcision is nothing; the only thing that counts is new creation" (Galatians 6:15). And when he is so changed, he plays his part in changing the world from a cesspit of corruption governed by the principle of death to the kingdom of heaven where all the brethren live together in the presence of God. The beautiful, short Psalm 133 expresses this vision perfectly.

> How good it is and how pleasant
> for brothers to live together!
> It is fragrant as oil poured over the head
> and falling over the beard,
> Aaron's beard, when the oil runs down
> over the collar of his vestments.
> It is like the dew of Hermon falling
> upon the hills of Zion.
>
> There the Lord bestows his blessing,
> life for evermore.

Another important biblical text that points to the necessity of a complete reconciliation with the source of suffering, and not merely its removal, is Numbers 21:4–9. This describes one of the frequent apostasies of the Israelites during their journey through the desert to the Promised Land. The Lord sent poisonous snakes among the people. These they bit so that many of them died. Once again there was general repentance, and the people asked Moses to plead with the Lord to rid them of the serpents. Moses interceded for them with God, and he was told to make a serpent of bronze and erect it as a standard, so that anyone who had been bitten should look upon it and recover. From this we learn that, until the source of suffering and death is confronted unflinchingly and its implications faced without fear, it will continue to cause destruction. But once this same affliction is lifted up in penitence and faith to God, it ceases to be destructive and becomes instead the agent of the person's healing. The things of darkness, once acknowledged to be mine, assume a transfigured radiance in the light of the healing power of the Holy Spirit. In John 3:14–15 we read that the Son of Man must be lifted up as the serpent was lifted up by Moses in the wilderness, so that anyone who has faith in Him may in Him possess eternal life. When the eyes are raised to Christ, they behold first the figure of a degraded man, crucified between two criminals — a reminder of the dread we all feel at the thought of disgrace, isolation and annihilation. But if they continue to watch, they see the resurrected Christ leaving His companions finally as He ascends to His eternal abode with the Father, so becoming available to all men even when two or three are gathered together in His name.

It is paradoxical that sickness is the way to healing and suffering the path to wholeness. What then is the authentic ministry of healing that should play a very important part in the spiritual life of the Church? It is that of sustaining the afflicted one during his period of suffering so that he can emerge a stronger, more compassionate person, able to bear the pain of the world. In this respect the problems that confront us come into two broad categories, the personal and the existential. *Personal problems* appertain to such immediate consideration as our state of health, our relationships with those close to us in the family and at work, our financial security, and the means of our employment. They can be modified and lightened, being within the scope of scientific and social understanding. The ministry of healing in this aspect of suffering embraces a vast range of disciplines extending from medical practice and its many ancillary branches, such as nursing and dietetics, through psychotherapy to education, economics and politics. It is important to realise that the agencies of healing are not restricted to those with medical skills, psychological knowledge or a paranormal healing gift. Each person is a potential minister of healing. (I prefer this title to that of "healer", which seems to place too much of the emphasis on the person and not enough on God, from whose Spirit all healing flows.)

The ministry of healing, as we see it in our present situation, is essentially a first-aid station for those who are afflicted with a personal problem of ill-health, family breakdown, poverty or unemployment. According to his problem, the specialised agency can prescribe the appropriate remedy, after which the person often feels better and functions more efficiently in his particular social environment. But it is doubtful whether he is a more whole, or integrated, individual, despite this amelioration of his problem. This criticism of the healing function, which embraces charismatic powers no less than orthodox medicine, in no way belittles the important role that its practitioners play in alleviating pain and soothing distress. The emergency treatment of suffering is the first step towards personal integration around the deep centre of the soul where God is known. But it is as likely to be followed by a relapse into complacency and selfishness as to guide the person into a heightened response to life's demands.

This criticism of much so-called spiritual healing is pertinent even to the ministry of Jesus. On one occasion He healed ten men with leprosy. Nine went out on their way without so much as coming back to thank Jesus and give praise to God. Only one, a foreigner, was filled with thanksgiving for what he had received (Luke 17:11–19). Jesus said to the man: "Stand up and go on your way, your faith has cured you." The other nine were also cured, but they were no nearer wholeness than before they had met Jesus. And even those who did respond positively to Jesus' healing touch by a change in attitude developed only slowly into full people. Where were they when their Lord was crucified? Jesus' healing work is to be seen as a manifestation of His love towards those who were diseased and rejected. It was a manifestation that the kingdom of God was upon the earth; it was a call to repentance and belief in the Gospel. The kingdom of God is above all an environment of love where all who reside are healed in body and integrated in soul. But it takes a long time — perhaps many lives — for the person to respond to that love and accept the gift of wholeness.

The *existential problems* that confront us are, unlike the purely personal ones, an inevitable aspect of our life on earth; they are inherent in existence itself. They have no easily applied answer, and we have to learn to live with them. They include such facts of life as ageing and death, the fight for survival in an overpopulated society, natural disasters that lead to the death of millions of people, and the law of entropy by which all energy-directed systems, including our world, run down and eventually perish. An application of this law is the present menacing fuel crisis that may indeed put an end to all future social and economic development. Life has its checks and balances. Through the great advances in medical science and more enlightened social policies, an increasing number of people are destined to live until they are very old. The result will be an intolerable degree of overcrowding with an increasing number of unemployed and a large population of retired, elderly people who have little constructive to do. And life becomes unbearable when one has nothing to look forward to, so that one day is indistinguishable from the next. Nature will, of course, solve the problem either by widespread famine or else by the sword. Even now the threat of nuclear destruction is the one restraining factor that prevents large-scale warfare in many parts of the world. No facile agency of healing can avert the tragedy in store for mankind — and therefore our world which has been placed under man's dominion. Only a complete change in man's fundamental outlook can save the world.

This change is embraced in the single quality of love, a word used so promiscuously to embrace every state of personal desire that it has ceased to have significant spiritual currency in our contemporary society. True love is essentially an experience in which the soul of one person vibrates in closest harmony with that of the other. They begin to function as one person, so close is the bond of unity. And yet it does not obliterate those differences in personality and outlook that are the glory of an individual person. Each has his own contribution to make, but this is achieved only when the person is secure in his social setting, needing neither to assert himself at the expense of others, nor fearing a threat to his identity by the mass of humanity in which he lies submerged. I have shown that this movement to personal integrity and authenticity is achieved only by the refining fire of suffering that transfigures all egoistical tendencies in the personality so that they become servants of the soul. Thereby the soul itself serves God as an integrated whole, and gives itself in service to the world. In the service of God there is alone perfect freedom, for in God we are accepted for what we are, and in that service we can see the other person as ourself. We learn the great lesson of spirituality that, in loving our neighbour as ourself, we see him in ourself and recognise the strong bonds of identification that unite all creatures. The disciples on the road to Emmaus recognised Christ in the stranger — at first, assuredly a very special stranger, the risen Lord, but ultimately in every stranger, because He is the eternal stranger. When we are lifted up to God on the cross, we start to be like Him, and we see that Christ is the power as well as the person who brings us all together, so that our love for each other is unitary. As St Paul puts it: "And because for us there is no veil over the face, we all reflect as in a mirror the splendour of the Lord; thus we are transfigured into his likeness, from splendour to splendour; such is the influence of the Lord who is Spirit" (II Corinthians 3:18).

It is at the heart of the paradox of the healing power of suffering that we begin to understand the true nature of the Antichrist who is always in our midst. He is the one who promises us deliverance from all our difficulties, who will solve all our problems for us. He makes our present lot so delightful that we desire nothing more than that our equilibrium may never be disturbed. He substitutes a worldly paradise for the kingdom of heaven. Antichrist is not a demonic figure typified in our own century by the person of a fascist or communist dictator or one of his henchmen. We have seen in Viktor Frankl's book *Man's Search for Meaning* how Nazi bestiality evoked saintliness in at least a few of its victims in the concentration camps of Europe, how their strength was made perfect in weakness. Some died praying that their torturers might attain forgiveness by virtue of their own sacrifice. In them we hear re-echoed Jesus' words on the cross: "Father, forgive them; they do not know what they are doing." These words are no more poignant than the witness of the world's saints of every age when they have been martyred for the sake of righteousness. Antichrist reveals himself much more subtly and plausibly than this. He appears as an outwardly enlightened man of apparent good nature and well-disposed to his fellows, who takes charge of the world and usurps the place of God. He organises the world into the form of an advanced welfare state and makes everyone happy provided they bow down and worship him. All who co-operate with him live pleasant, uneventful lives, have plenty of possessions, and strive for the maintenance of their present status. Their inner eye is no longer lifted up to the Figure on the cross, who is the way, the truth and the life in God. Therefore they are not themselves transformed. They remain comfortable, complacent people, selfish and blind to the greater world, living like intelligent animals. They do not respond to the existential problems of life until they disappear, like the followers of Korah, swallowed up by the earth that splits and opens to receive their mortal bodies (Numbers 16:31). This is the way of Antichrist, that great deceiver, who promises us all the kingdoms of the world in their glory if we will only fall down and do him homage (Matthew 4:9).

The way to wholeness can be likened to removing skin after skin from an onion until the succulent core is revealed. Every skin of selfish desire has to be shed before the pearl within is discovered. This is the seed of God deeply placed in the soul, and, by a miracle of grace, it has pity on the outer discarded skins. It flows out to them in love, transfigures them to a new resurrection in which they give of themselves to the world, and makes their previously selfish desire now one for universal redemption. Our inner serpent, the selfish desire nature which is the accuser that casts its menacing shadow over the whole of our inner life, is raised up, transfigured on the cross of our affliction and becomes a life-giving power in the world.

There are no short cuts in our growth into spiritual beings. This is another way of affirming the slow emergence of the awakened person from the darkness of hell to the light of God's creative power. To be sure, there are many practitioners of the occult and purveyors of exotic meditation techniques around us in the world today who proffer instant panaceas to the gullible and unwise. But neither they nor their followers show the stature of a fully realised person. They remain trapped in the confines of their particular teaching or technique which subtly assumes an absolute authority in their lives. There is also the type of person who very properly responds deeply to the spiritual teachings of all the great religious traditions. He feels that, at heart, they are all saying the same thing, and that love is the basis of life. All this is surely true enough, but until one has given of oneself uncompromisingly to a particular way and tasted the fruits in one's own life, one will be merely scratching the surface of authentic existence. Such a purveyor of religions applauds the spirituality of the saints with his mind, but takes good care not to commit himself to knowing that spirituality in his own life. If he were to take the plunge into the depths of reality, only then would he emerge a changed person, divested of all superficial complacency by the penetrating, healing rays of suffering. It is only on that level that one can begin to appreciate the transcendental unity that underlies all authentic religious traditions.

How best can those who are undergoing spiritual pain be helped? One takes it for granted, of course, that suffering of a remediable type should be dealt with according to its source, whether physical, mental or social. The body should be revitalised and the person should be reinstated in his appropriate social setting, properly fed, clothed and housed. Until people have learned the elementary lessons of hygiene, they will never revere the sanctity of the body they have been given. Until people learn to respect their fellows and assimilate the golden rule — always treat others as you would like them to treat you (Matthew 7:12) — they will not know the holiness of personal relationships, and all partnerships, extending from collaboration in work to the sacrament of marriage, will founder on the sands of boredom, disillusionment and mistrust. Until the spiritual law is grasped, especially the law of supply — set your mind on God's kingdom and His justice before everything else, and all the rest will come to you as well (Matthew 6:33) — there can be no lasting material happiness and progress.

The intense pain of the soul is, however, something apart from this. It cannot be communicated easily to others, and only those who have travelled the same path can be of authentic help to the one in darkness. As I have already indicated, this pain is a compound of nameless, relentless fear, a sense of despair which has a personal as well as a cosmic component, and an agonising depression that annuls all attempts at work or recreation. This depression is, in part, the "accidie" that is known to assail spiritual aspirants — dry periods of sloth and torpor which are an outer manifestation of an inner despair that renders all spiritual effort futile. The personal component of the dark night of the spirit is God's way of depriving the soul of everything save a direct knowledge of Himself, and that in the dark emptiness of His incomprehensibility rather than in the light of His love. The dark face of God reflects the darkness of the world that its creatures have wrought through their self-centred appropriation of its substance. One has to suffer with God the Son, who was made flesh and dwelt among us in great humility, before one can know the uncreated light of the Holy Spirit and glimpse the unutterable splendour of the Father.

The cosmic component of the dark night of the spirit is the

occluding psychic despair that descends like a black pall on the soul of the sufferer. It is the psychic darkness, previously described, which forms the basis of the collective pain of mankind, that annihilating power which Jesus had to encounter on His own in the Garden of Gethsemane, and which he overcame with love in the hell to which He descended after His crucifixion.

Spiritual suffering is overcome not by alleviation but by penetration. This is the great difference between the relief of personal problems and the healing of the whole person. If a personal problem is relieved, the sufferer emerges with felicity into a realm of ease and repose, which, by the very nature of life, is only an illusion. In due course he will be assailed by another problem, be it of ill-health, mental breakdown, or a shattering of some deep relationship which will leave him bereft of comfort and assurance. The healing of the whole person entails a resurrection of all that was ailing or incomplete in him, so that he emerges a renewed being, reflecting in himself the risen Lord. One has, as it were, to immerse oneself in full awareness and with absolute "onepointedness" into the suffering, so that it ceases to be separate from one but instead becomes one's closest associate. As one knows it, so one begins to accept it; as one accepts it, so one begins to love it. Perfect love banishes fear (I John 4:18).

It follows that the best way of healing a person in spiritual distress is to be with him constantly. This means a faithful witness to his need in the Spirit of God. One prays for him without ceasing, remembering him in one's intercessions and upholding him in one's thoughts at all times. He should also be assured of one's physical presence, both in direct encounter and by the medium of the telephone and the written word, as often as is expedient. It is not that we have much positive guidance to give him — only those who have emerged from the pit of travail themselves are reliable guides, and an inner wisdom informs their witness with a strong eloquent silence — so much as that our presence affords a constant source of strength and love to a soul isolated by psychic darkness. We dare not sleep when even the meanest of our brethren is in pain; we must be awake when Christ is crucified in the form of all who suffer and are cast out of respectable society. He is always identified with the victims of society's cruelty, and we show ourselves most authentically as spiritual beings when we are seen with Him in the slums, the prisons, the hospitals and the concentration camps.

Prayer is an essential act in the relief of spiritual suffering. It has two components: intercession for the one in pain and an even deeper intercession for those who are physically dead but whose souls are in torment in the life beyond death. It is to this subject of healing prayer that we must give our final attention.

Meditation

The person who is approaching wholeness is able to confront the full panoply of life's vicissitudes with realism, courage, and faith. He has no ready-made answers, no esoteric wisdom that deflects from his own judgement, but he advances fearlessly through the darkness of unknowing confident of the eternal presence of the One Who resurrected matter to spirit and conquered death by love.

16
Healing Prayer

Prayer is the elevation of the mind to God; its apogee is the act of contemplation whereby the human soul is infused by God's spirit so that it partakes of the divine energies. These energies, typified by the uncreated light of God, bring the soul ever nearer to its divine source. We have already read the doctrine from St Paul: "And because for us there is no veil over the face, we all reflect as in a mirror, the splendour of the Lord; thus we are transfigured into His likeness, from splendour to splendour; such is the influence of the Lord who is Spirit" (II Corinthians 3:18). We believe that we pray, but in fact it is the Holy Spirit who is the foundation of our praying. When we are sufficiently humbled of our usual conceit and can listen in rapt attention to God, He speaks to us and through us, leading us in the adventure of praying. There are as many ways of praying as there are people who pray; assuredly the one Spirit prays through all of us, but we add our own distinctive flavour to the prayer uttered, and this contributes its potency to the product. "Taste then, and see that the Lord is good" (Psalm 34:8).

It is God's will that all creatures should be healed: of this I have no doubt. But I also have no doubt that the healing of God is *of a different order* from that envisaged by man, even by most healers who work on a charismatic basis. We look for an outward sign of improvement, but God sees into the heart. We desire relief and a return to normal activity, but God looks for a transfigured person. "For my thoughts are not your thoughts, and your ways are not my ways. For as the heavens are higher than the earth, so are my ways higher than your ways and my thoughts than your thoughts" (Isaiah 55:8–9). Before we have had time to articulate our prayers even in our minds, God knows their content. He knows what our needs are before we ask Him (Matthew 6:8); He, in fact, makes their satisfaction possible by leading us into that state of inner quiet where we can receive the Holy Spirit. "When you pray, go into a room by yourself, shut the door, and pray to your Father who is there in the secret place; and your Father who sees what is in secret will reward you" (Matthew 6:6). When our will coincides with the will of God, a state that is most fully attainable during the act of contemplation, God informs our will of the part it is to play in the healing of all people. In this way we become true ministers of healing.

When we pray for another person we should first attain a state of inner quiet in which we can be attentive to the divine will. "Let be then: learn that I am God" (Psalm 46:10). Prayer of any real intensity (which is rather different from reciting set prayers) starts with silence before God — just as in any deep communication with another person we should first of all be quiet and "listen" to him, and that not only with our ears but with our whole being. This silence is contemplative prayer. In the silence we are at one, not only with God the Holy Spirit, but also with the spirit of all those who are in need. Then, when we remember these people, the power of God passes through our spirit to theirs, for in prayer there is a spiritual bond between all creatures. The bond is the work of God's Holy Spirit. In intercessory prayer, we interpose ourselves between God and the person for whom we are praying; it is a mystery of God's courtesy to us that He uses us in this great work of healing; indeed, it is amazing that creatures as imperfect as we are should play such an important part in God's healing work for the whole world. "What is man that thou shouldst remember him, mortal man that thou shouldst care for him? Yet thou hast made him little less than a god, crowning him with glory and honour" (Psalm 8:4–5).

The essence of all real healing work — and this includes our work in alleviating the suffering that is a necessary part of a person's growth into a full human being — is to be an agent of love. As I have stressed on more than one occasion, the precious fruit of suffering is a capacity of love on a universal scale without ego-centred dependence on the loved one, an attitude that makes itself known in a demanding, possessive relationship that enslaves the object of our affection. If the person in travail meets unreserved love, his sufferings are modified, and he can come to an appreciation of the meaning of his pain much more rapidly. Thus the healing power of love accelerates the necessary cleansing work of suffering and brings the sufferer closer to his true self much more immediately than would be possible in a cold, uncaring atmosphere. The love a minister of healing like Jesus radiates is the first experience of divine love the one in travail will know, and will eventually give to others when he emerges from the darkness of psychical gloom and enters into the light of God's creative purpose.

To be a real minister of healing there are two strict prerequisites: an ardent love of God and a capacity to love one's fellow creatures. This is, in fact, a summary of the two great commandments — loving the Lord our God with all our being, and loving our neighbour as ourself. When one prays for someone in need, one lifts him up to God in the silence of contemplative prayer, and then one remembers his particular physical illness or mental distress. It is more important to embrace the sufferer with unconditional love than to pray for his relief from a particular illness or difficulty. Once he is filled with the Spirit of God, a deeper healing will occur than anything we may demand. By this I do not suggest that we should not pray to God for our personal needs to be met or our inner questions answered, or even more so that those for whom we are interceding should not be similarly helped. What I am saying is this, that the seeking aspect of petitionary and intercessory prayer is a logical sequel to the contemplative prayer which puts us and those for whom we care in God's loving embrace. Only when we are supported by the everlasting arms of God can healing occur on the various levels of the personality. The spirit inspires the soul and purifies it; the informed soul infuses the mind and renews the body. In this way there comes about a full psychosomatic healing. It may well be that the particular trouble is not removed — certainly St Paul's "thorn in the flesh" was not healed although he begged the Lord on three occasions to rid him of it. It was probably a severe physical pain of some kind, and Paul was told: "My grace is all you need; power comes to its full strength in weakness." St Paul follows this with the important dictum that he prefers to find his joy and pride in the very things that are his weakness, and then the power of Christ will come and rest upon him (II Corinthians 12:7–9).

This, of course, does not mean that we should not seek relief from our travail in the deepest prayer, but that we must be obedient to God's final word, remembering that while we desire instant relief, God wills our growth into mature manhood, measured by nothing less than the full stature of Christ (Ephesians 4:13). The theme of this book is that suffering is an essential part of this process. Only when we have learned the particular lesson that our travail is here to teach us can we put away the past pain and enter new fields of endeavour. In the end it is not so much the pain that is terrible as the apparent meaninglessness that surrounds most suffering like an impenetrable, black pall. When we can begin to see our own suffering as a part of universal disorder, and can visualise the raising up of the whole world "from the shackles of mortality and its entry upon the liberty and splendour of the children of God" (to quote St Paul at his most inspired in Romans 8:21), then only is our condition invested with supernatural significance. Only then can we play our part in this liberation of the universe from the law of death and disintegration that ends all natural processes.

We have to come to terms with our own involvement in and responsibility for the disorder that appears to dominate the world. Every selfish action, every unkind word, every destructive thought has its repercussions not only on those

around us but also in the wider psychic environment in which
we live as spiritual beings. And what is disordered psychically
will make its impact felt in the material world. Our own
thoughtless attitudes play their part in fostering man's inhumanity to his fellows. I also firmly believe that man's psychic
disorder has a deep effect on the conditions of the earth, so
intimately connected are the human emotions and the phenomena of the natural world. We tend to blame God for not
intervening to arrest the tragedies of the world, but these are
largely of our own creation. They are also, no doubt, a product
of the demonic powers that reside in the psychic realms, and
which feed on negative emotional forces that emanate from
psychologically disturbed human beings. This consideration
brings us to another, deeper aspect of healing prayer — that
which involves the psychic world in which the "dead" live and
work towards their sanctification in God.

The question of prayers for the dead has already been
broached in connection with the passage in II Maccabees
12:38–45. It would seem from what has been imparted to
many sensitive people, that some who have died are often
closer in psychical communion to those of us still alive in the
flesh than to the Communion of Saints who inhabit the vast
world of heaven. This applies especially to people who have
lived selfish, corrupt, cruel lives. Their centre of attention had
seldom moved much beyond their physical bodies and the
desire nature of the ego while they lived in this world. When
the time had come for them to quit their mortal bodies, the
immaterial mind-soul was so undeveloped that it hovered
around the psychic environment of the earth, being unable, or
unwilling, to move into its proper milieu in the life beyond
death. I am now speaking of hell, which is not a place but a
psychic atmosphere of dereliction, isolation and purposeless,
repetitive motion. To the type of person that is so sensuous
and hedonistic that he cannot lift his awareness above the
level of his mortal body, death is a shattering experience. His
physical moorings have been loosened, and he drifts aimlessly

in the lower psychical ("astral") world seeking desperately for some body of flesh and bone to which he can become anchored. This "discarnate entity" can cause grave disturbances especially to people with strong psychic sensitivity. While spiritualists may attempt to get into direct contact with such an unhappy soul by what is called a "rescue circle", a much better and far less dangerous means of approach is through intercessory prayer and the celebration of a Requiem Mass. The importance of prayers for the dead cannot be over-emphasised, and it is the entities without faith that need our solicitude far more than those who have lived and died in faith. Indeed, we read in Wisdom 3:1–4: "The souls of the just are in God's hand and torment shall not touch them. In the eyes of foolish men they seemed to be dead; their departure was reckoned a defeat, and their going a disaster. But they are in peace." The peace that the writer describes is not a state of repose but one of intimate communion with God in which all the good things of eternal life are enjoyed. It is clear that we need the help of the faithful departed much more than they our prayers! They are already playing their part in the Communion of Saints.

If the necessity for intercessory prayer is accepted for the indifferent discarnate entities that populate the intermediate zones close to our earth, how much more important it must be for those really evil people who, in their lives, killed millions of their fellow men and filled the world with hatred and violence! In their psychic hell they are in blackness and enveloped in the world's hatred, especially the loathing of the descendants of their victims and perhaps of some of the victims also. This psychic atmosphere of evil is not only appalling in itself; it also casts its noxious influence over the whole cosmos. It was this life-destroying miasma that Jesus had to encounter face to face in His supreme agony in the Garden of Gethsemane, and which, I believe, afflicts, though to a lesser extent, many sensitive people today with episodes of unaccountable depression. Fortunately for us, the risen Christ is available to

help us in the necessary encounter with the world's accumulated sin; for Him to come to us, however, we have to pray.
Only thus may we open the inner door on which He knocks
perpetually, asking to be admitted to His rightful place in our
own being. This is the apex of the soul where the spirit lies as a
pearl of great price. The encounter with this psychic darkness
is an inevitable trial on the probationary path of all who are
called to higher spiritual service, and its end is the raising up of
the evil to perpetual light; the transforming power is love, by
which alone redemption is effected.

It therefore follows that healing prayer should not be confined only to the living but must be extended to the dead. We
should remember in love not only those who have lived good
lives while on earth, but also the criminals, the torturers, the
persecutors and those who have seduced the world in their
time with vain philosophies and noxious ideologies. The work
of intercession for the most evil men now departed this life is
assuredly a dedicated ministry. I would not recommend it to
those who are unschooled in the life of prayer. They are best
employed in remembering people in special present need. But
those whose life is centred on God, and to whom prayer is as
essential for the life of the soul as breathing is for that of the
body, should pray ceaselessly for all souls in misery in the
outer reaches of the life beyond death. Contemplative com-
munities have a special responsibility in this work, and so also
do those many elderly people who feel that their lives, lacking
physical purpose, now have no further use. Indeed, this is a
very special service for those who only stand and wait for their
summons to pass through the gate of death to enter the new
life that lies ahead of them. The future of our planet depends
in no small measure on the healing of the psychic atmosphere
that envelops it, because the power of the Holy Spirit has to
penetrate this layer before it can energise the physical world
with life. As the psychic world is cleansed, so will ennobling
thoughts enter the minds of those who are burdened with the
government of great nations. Then they will be able to grasp

their common humanity and the fatherhood of the Almighty, no matter how they envisage Him or what name they give to Him. And then the Spirit of Christ, who gave up His life to save the world, will penetrate their spirit also and renunciation will take the place of the strivings for self-aggrandisement that typify natural man. Demands for victory will be swallowed up in universal reconciliation, and the greatest will be the servant of all.

It should also be emphasised that healing prayer must begin with the person who prays. I cannot be an authentic minister of healing so long as my private life is disordered and my present relationships at home or at my work are unsatisfactory. "Why do you look at the speck of sawdust in your brother's eye, with never a thought for the great plank in your own? Or how can you say to your brother 'Let me take the speck out of your eye' when all the time there is the plank in your own? You hypocrite! First take the plank out of your own eye, and then you will see clearly to take the speck out of your brother's" (Matthew 7:3–5). It is futile for me to pray earnestly for peace in faraway places while there is no peace in me or in my closest relationships with others. Only when I am at peace in myself will that peace radiate from me to my surroundings and start to heal all those in need. Only then will my prayers on behalf of the world be effective, for an attitude of benevolence and love, such as peace engenders, can have profound psychic effects far away from its original human source. That peace is a fruit of suffering long and gaining an inner wisdom that sees beyond immediate personal gratification.

Another rather unlikely component of true healing prayer is a sense of humour. This glorious fruit of suffering comes when we are shown the immensity of God's grace and the insignificance of our personal complaints. I could well imagine that when Job came fully to himself after his shattering encounter with the Creator he burst out in laughter as he saw himself and his previous way of life in the context of God's infinity. When we encounter the rigid limits of conventional wisdom in juxtaposition with the immensity of universal truth, we respond not rationally but mystically, in a paean of laughter. No wonder both Abraham and Sarah laughed when they were told by God that they were to be the parents of Isaac, for it was logically impossible for the aged Sarah to conceive a child. The fool and the clown are divine symbols. They are the way in which logic-weary man transcends the limit of the possible and enters a kingdom where a little child is master of all. Only those who accept the kingdom of God like a child can enter it (Mark 10:15). The kingdom is attained not by violence but by the acceptance of things as they are. The oil that lubricates the wheels of life and moves the cumbersome human organism to its place in heaven is the blessed balm of humour. Only one who has overcome himself in the fire of affliction can laugh unaffectedly at life's vicissitudes. And he can pray effectively also, because he has learned how to get himself out of the way and be an instrument for God's healing power. There is a lightness about true spirituality that brings us into communion with the angels and the blessed ones. "Thus speaks the high and exalted one, whose name is holy, who lives for ever: I dwell in a high and holy place with him who is broken and humble in spirit, to revive the spirit of the humble, to revive the courage of the broken" (Isaiah 57:15). I would think that the broken ones in the twentieth-century prison camps throughout the world are revived through the courage born of celestial humour, for when we are nothing, we are also one with God.

Should we pray for the demonic powers that influence the world from other spheres as fallen members of the angelic hierarchy? Should we intercede for the personified power of evil that is called the devil? It seems best that we should concern ourselves first of all with our own business, which is the transfiguration of human society and the creatures of our world. If we play our part properly in this limited realm, it is more than likely that the powers of the cosmos will attain greater attunement among themselves than at present. Then the great cosmic fellowship, of which we also are a part, may work towards universal harmony.

Despite the terrible times that are upon us at present, this great day of peace and love may be nearer than we dare to hope. For then we shall be like Him, because we shall see Him as He is.

Meditation

Let the healing grace of your love, O Lord, so transform me that I may play my part in the transfiguration of the world from a place of suffering, death and corruption to a realm of infinite light, joy, and love. Make me so obedient to your Spirit that my life may become a living prayer and a witness to your unfailing presence.

The Summing-Up

Jesus said: "The hour has come for the Son of Man to be glorified. In truth, in very truth I tell you, a grain of wheat remains a solitary grain unless it falls into the ground and dies; but if it dies, it bears a rich harvest. The man who loves himself is lost, but he who hates himself in this world will be kept safe for eternal life" (John 12:23–25). This is the paradox of life and death; the reconciling factor is suffering, which changes the ego-self from something that is ephemeral and insubstantial to the rock-like permanence of the true self whose home is in God. Not only are we to change from mere outer dross to refined gold, but we are to lift up every creature as the serpent in the wilderness was raised up on high as a bronze standard, so that it might become an object of healing.

In the words of the *Bhagavadgita* (11:55): "He who does work for Me, he who looks upon Me as his goal, he who worships Me, free from attachment, he who is free from enmity to all creatures, he goes to Me." These stern requirements form the spiritual life to which all aspirants dedicate themselves. But they are fulfilled in life itself by living more perfectly day by day. The way of perfection is by suffering. By slow attrition everything inessential to salvation is worn down. By love all is restored, renewed and sanctified. The solitary grain that has apparently died is resurrected as a universe of life, that sings of the eternal glory of the Creator, Redeemer and Sanctifier.